A Thousand Years on a Chiltern Farm

The Story of Grove Farm Chesham

by A.S. (Tony) Harman

With contributions from

Dr Arnold Baines
Thor Harman
Jennifer Moss
Roy & Anne Paton
and members of Chess Valley Archaeological & Historical Society

Published in 1999 by
M R Harman
Field Top
Orchard Leigh
Chesham
Bucks HP5 3QE

Copyright © A.S. Harman and contributors 1999

All rights reserved. No part of this publication may be reproduced, stored in a retrieval system, or transmitted in any form or by any means, electronic, mechanical, photocopying, recording or otherwise, without the prior permission of the publisher and copyright holder.

The author has asserted the moral right to be identified as the author of this work.

British Library Cataloguing in Publication Data.

A catalogue record for this book is available from the British Library.

ISBN   0 9537421 0 5

Production   Merrin Molesworth, Chesham, Bucks

Printed in Great Britain by Stanley Mason Printer Ltd, Amersham, Bucks

Outside Front Cover: Grove as it may have appeared in the year 1500, by Laurence Pearce

A Thousand Years on a Chiltern Farm
The Story of Grove Farm Chesham
by Tony Harman

Contents

A Thousand Years at Grove

Epilogue

What the Records Tell Us about Grove
Pre-history to the 11th Century
1. The 12th and 13th centuries: the De Brocs
2. The 14th century. Walter Langton
3. Later 14th century and 15th & 16th centuries: the Cheynes
4. The 17th, 18th and 19th centuries

Appendices

Walter de La Grave's two virgates
The fields of Grove
When did that happen?

Key to References

About the Contributors
About the Author

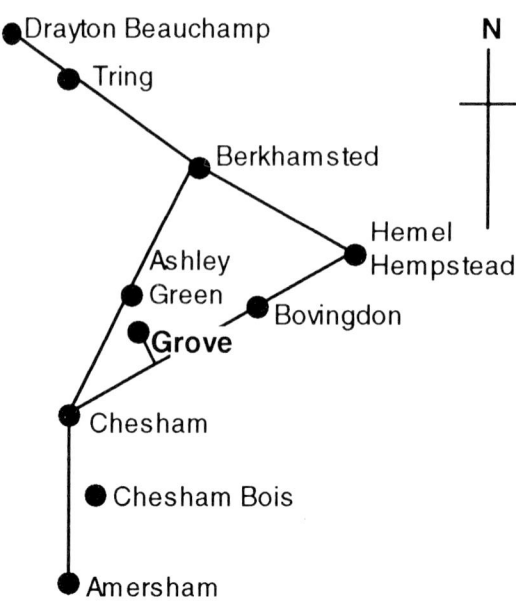

Figure 1　Location of Grove

A Thousand Years at Grove

by Tony Harman

Earthworks are always mysterious, whether they are huge national monuments like Silbury Hill or small farm moats. Why did everybody, or anybody, go to such trouble, for many people must have been involved? The farm moats are mainly accounted for by the prosaic process of collecting water where there were no springs. Others, the experts tell me, were mere showing off by the householder that he had a moated site on which he lived. Nothing to do with defence, but more like the garden gnomes in the suburban home.

I became aware of our moat when I was about nine years old, when my father bought Grove Farm. The moat seemed to me enormously big. Also, it is double, which rules out that it was there for collecting water; but it remained a mystery. There was a stone building in the middle of it of which some of the old locals said: "Oh, that was done by them monks", and in staunchly Protestant Buckinghamshire a monk was a very sinister thing! They didn't go near the place at night for fear of a ghost of the monks. They really didn't. Others mumbled about "them old Romans". Of course, somewhere or other there were written records, we just didn't know where they were.

As a small boy I used to sit on the bank of the moat and imagine what it was like when it was being built. I could see men working in the bottom with barrows and baskets and ox-carts hauling out the clay. There were ramps on the corners because the moat is square and that's where the ox-carts were drawing out the clay and heaping it in big heaps to the west of the site. There were women sorting the stones from the clay for re-use on the building. The people I saw in my imagination were the people who still existed in the area. They were the farm workers on the farm who I saw working in the moat, digging. It was the women who picked the stones in the fields in the 1920's, or earlier, who were sorting the stones from the heaps outside the moat. And I suppose, in that, I was right - it was the ancestors of these people who did it.

At the point where the entrance crosses the inner moat, there are foundations of two flint towers, very thick walls, not very high. People were still, in my time, helping themselves to stone from the wall to fill holes in the drives, easier than picking them up in the fields!

Figure 2   Who dug this earthwork and when? Part of the north side of the moat, looking east.

I don't know how high the towers had been, but you could still see the rough shape and, as we got older and stronger, we decided to investigate. We started to dig out from the northern one rubbish that had filled it over many years. The area around the building had been used as a stack yard and the waste material from the thrashing, short straw and chaff had blown into the tower, filled it and rotted down so that digging was easy. We found a step going down. We found another step going down and, in great excitement, a third and a fourth step, and then nothing but a dirt floor. So, after an interval to recover our enthusiasm, we started on the other tower. That was filled with stone and there we moved the stone from the base, expecting to find steps and perhaps a dirt floor again, but we didn't. We found a very small well, only about 18" wide and beautifully faced off, with knapped flints but filled with big stones. Laboriously, we hauled some of them out. They were a worked stone, a chamfered stone, obviously having come from a building of some sort. Unfortunately we never saved them, principally because when we got the hole, with great difficulty, out to two to three feet deep a cow slipped its hind quarters in one night. It was hauled out with much struggling and we were very unpopular on the farm and were ordered immediately to refill the well.

George Larkin, a Baptist lay preacher who was a farm foreman, came on the scene and said to us very gravely and mysteriously: "You know, you don't want to look in the past. You only find things that's bad. The people who used to live up here were up to no good, otherwise they wouldn't have wanted a moat anyway, would they? So leave it alone and think about the future." He then went on to say "And I remember when I was young, opening up the floor of an old

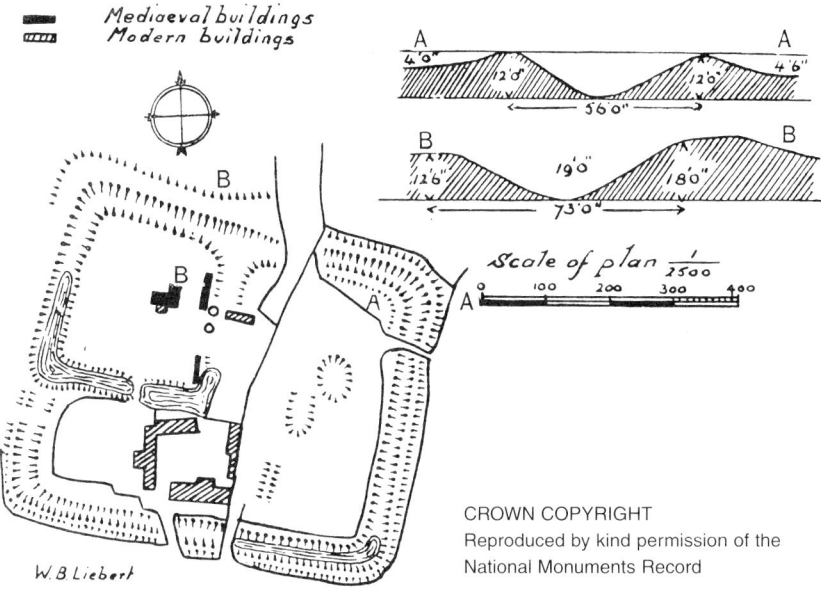

Figure 3 Homestead Moat at Grove Farm, RCHM 1912

house where I lived at St. Leonard's, and what did they find, bones, bones. Somebody had been buried there and you might have found something like that. Leave it alone, think about the future, not the past."

The building within the moat was always described as the Chapel. It had been so described on the first Ordnance Survey maps, largely because there was an arched stone doorway which looked like a chapel door, but little other evidence except for 'them old monks' again. The interior of the building, insofar as it remained, was high, very high and was used for storage of various kinds at various times. Nobody questioned but that it had been a chapel. I kept looking at it and something seemed wrong and by constant looking I realised there had been one, or in places two, upper floors. You could see where the beams had been cut out of the walls leaving stumps. Somehow that didn't look as if it had been a medieval chapel. The niche high up on the north-eastern corner, which some said had housed an image of some sort, was obviously - when you looked at it - a doorway into something which was no longer there. It was quite obvious when you looked at it in detail. So it had been a house of some sort. Certainly not built as a chapel, if ever used as one. It stayed on the map as a chapel and in everybody's conversation it was referred to as a chapel. For many years nothing else was discovered or revealed, except that in the middle 1920's, an expert on medieval Bucks, came to have lunch with my mother and suggested that it had belonged to somebody called Adam de la Grove in the middle ages. He had got almost everything wrong because Adam owned the Grove at Chalfont. In his time our place hadn't yet been described as the Grove, it was 'la Grave'.

Figure 4 Home to a solitary bull – east front of Grove in 1948

The building continued in limited use, storing from time to time hay, straw, corn, potatoes and once a lonely bull living safely confined within its thick walls. A little while before the Second World War, I was approached by somebody who said they were acting on behalf of the government, needing storage space for emergency supplies. I agreed the use and, within days, lorry loads of corned beef in boxes of tins arrived and the building was filled almost to the eaves. After the War had started, this was removed in small amounts until all had gone. During the whole of that time, there were no locks on the doors, indeed, there weren't any doors really, only broken pieces of doors, and yet absolutely not one tin was missing when they came to check up.

Too busy on other things to find out, it wasn't until the Sixties that further evidence of the past appeared.

Figure 5 Two phases of construction can be seen in this view from the west. The corner masonry changes to brick and the flints in the wall are different, 1999

In 1960, a very old established firm of solicitors, Francis & How of Chesham, sent me a bundle of papers which they said must refer to my property. Sure enough, it was a series of documents relating to part of the farm, commencing with the gift from one John Partridge of the Grove, to his daughter when she got married and tracing the history of a particular field right through to the beginning of the 19th century. John Partridge was easily traceable in the local Parish register and, obligingly, he appeared to have put his initials JP at the base of the putlog[1] stones in the upper part of the wall. But this conclusion of mine could be wrong because scientific evidence now shows that the roof was put on around 1499, some 80 years or so before John Partridge. Perhaps he renewed it or something of that sort. It then jumped out at me that the first seven feet of the wall were of faced flints from an earlier period and above that the wall is of much rougher construction made of bits and pieces of re-used stone, new flint and some brick. The new fact which came from John Partridge's papers which I didn't immediately recognise, was that he described it as 'late manor of the Grove'. That was the first mention I saw of it ever having been a manor.[2]

---

1 The stones let into a wall to hold scaffold boards.
2 The manor was the hub of medieval village life. Under the jurisdiction of the Lord of the Manor, his tenants regulated their farming and social life and interpreted their local customs. The manor court was the place where most local disputes about tenancies, services and dues were heard and settled.

Again in the sixties, when all the world started looking to its own past, looking up its ancestry, finding out its roots, somebody came to see me from the Buckinghamshire Archaeological Society. He walked around and said "You have got a splendid Tudor roof on that building; it shouldn't be allowed to fall down". So the question arose as to how to preserve it and it was decided that the only way was to turn the building back into a house. At that time, one had to get the agreement of the Ministry of Works and they sent down somebody to inspect it who expressed the opinion that the whole site could even have been an Iron Age camp which somebody had tried to enlarge and develop in the Middle Ages; not so much tried to, but succeeded, in doing. His theory was subsequently laughed to scorn by other experts who said, because it was square, it could be nothing to do with the Iron Age, who always did things round (which I have since found not to be true). The same person from the Ministry laid down rules for us. We could turn it back into a house, but nothing must be faked. Where parts had fallen and roofs had collapsed, their replacements must be modern. The only thing we were allowed to do was to get stone of the same type as the arch at the front doorway, to replace that because it was collapsing. Samples taken revealed it had come all the way from Tisbury in Wiltshire - a long way in the Middle Ages by horse and wagon. So duly the work was done and the building was returned to use as a house.

Figure 6 A 15th century window frame still in use. The stonework is rebated inside for shutters

Work started also on the garden which had been overgrown with rubbish. Everywhere you went you found stone foundations, walls - in one case a rectangular pit, quite well plastered on the inside (it is difficult to imagine the use). These foundations were everywhere. So there had been something much bigger on the site which needed investigation.

While this had been going on, I had become interested in the Buckinghamshire Record Society which exists to publish (generally once a year) transcriptions of early records from the Middle Ages (sometimes a bit later) taxation records, call up records, that sort of thing, and I avidly searched their books for references to my own property. I found precious little at that stage, precious little.

Walking the farm for the whole of my life, and working the fields for most of it, I had always been intrigued by the differences between them. Some quite rectangular, some very oddly shaped with curved or crooked hedges, just odd shapes which seemed to have no reason, and it gradually sank in that these must relate to how they were cleared, because in early days when you were doing most of the work by hand, straight lines didn't mean much at all. You cleared what was easy to clear and that meant diverting around big trees, it meant probably meeting head-on a neighbour who was clearing, and arguing about exactly which

Figure 7   Nothing must be faked! The view shows the 1960s wing that replaced a wooden extension

way to go. So hedge lines representing division between properties or areas cleared were quite irregular. Other parts of the farm where there were straight hedge lines, and sometimes ditches, must relate to an organised clearance when the land was all in the hands of one owner, in other words, an estate of some sort.

And so to the County Archives to see if anything could be found, just looking for dates of enclosure and simple things like that. I came across a reference to Walter de la Grave who, in 1128, was granted manorial rights over

Figure 8 The trees from which these timbers were cut in about 1499 were growing when Richard III was king

two virgates of land.[3] No other information as to who Walter was at that stage, just Walter de la Grave. Now I was soon told (by an expert) that de la Grave meant 'of the ditch', so the moat or ditch was already there, or at least part of it, and Walter was living near it. Of course this raised the question of how did the moat or ditch get to be there in 1128. Irritatingly I couldn't find any document or reference that would allow me to identify Grove or la Grave positively earlier than that. However Dr Arnold Baines has kindly contributed a paper (which appears on page 26) that draws parallels with other early manors.

But so far as our Grove is concerned, two virgates of land, how does one trace that? From the Ordnance Survey map, looked at as a whole, it stuck out a mile. A little bit out from the moat, there was a rectangular area enclosed by ditches and hedges, pretty well square, enclosing just over 60 acres of land. That is two virgates. So we had got the right Grove because that had been in doubt. There are Grove Farms all over the place, probably several of them with ditches, but this Walter lived at our Grove with his two virgates of land. Not very much, a very small manor and now partly woods. So those woods were later woods, replanted, because in fact they had been chalk quarries.

Eyesight having gone, I wasn't able to research any further, only to speculate and go through the publications of the Record Society with somebody else reading to me - could anything be found? Not much.

Then my grandson Thor Harman, was able to take over from me and go to the Public Records Office in London, as well as to the County Archives and find out when the property was mentioned. And a lot came out. There was a complete record of ownership after 1128. Pretty standard stuff, just owners, and incidentally the first mention in 1206 of Whelpley Hill, the nearest hamlet, but

---

3   In the old measures of area a virgate in this part of the country was thirty acres. An acre was roughly what a man with an ox team could plough in a day.

mainly things about one family called de Broc who owned Grove for a long period. Walter may have been Walter de Broc or called himself that. There is just a possibility, that's all, that Walter de la Grave was Walter de Broc - place names and family names are hopelessly mixed up together throughout history and to this day (particularly in Scotland) farmers are frequently referred to by the name of their farm and not by their patronym. Whether or not he had been de la Grave, the de Brocs were a large and powerful family. They turned out to have property, not just in Buckinghamshire, but in Northamptonshire, in Godalming in Surrey and to have once been custodians of Saltwood Castle in Kent. De Brocs were closely involved with the assassination of Archbishop Thomas Becket in 1170. One of them helped the assassins to break into the Cathedral though he did not take part in the murder.

It all reads as though they had great influence with King Henry II and had with others, in modern language, wound him up against Becket so that he uttered the fatal words which are always quoted: "Who will rid me of this turbulent priest". Curiously, it seems to have been the King who did the penance and he did not demand the same of the de Brocs, so far as we know. We don't know if the de Brocs were Saxons who had, so to speak, cuddled up to Normans or whether they were in fact Normans themselves. The word Broc means brook in Anglo-Saxon or, alternatively, badger, sometimes. Whatever they were, the de Brocs had

Figure 9 Back in use as a house – the east front of Grove in 1999

obtained enormous influence in a short space of time between 1066 and the time of Becket, and continued this influence for quite a long while afterwards.

Unfortunately, from my point of view and what I was trying to investigate, there is no record of how the de Brocs managed the agricultural side of their estates. Land transactions relating to the manor of Wingrave in Bucks, to the manor de la Grave (our manor), and to Hundridge manor also near Chesham, as well as in the other counties, are all recorded. In the Bodleian Library in Oxford, there is a letter from Becket to a monastery situated in a de Broc area in Bucks, sometime before his assassination. So there is a very close relationship, but in spite of all their properties they were knights not barons and their property in Bucks would have been under the feudal control of the Earls of Oxford. Perhaps that is why they were never made barons or earls or something of that sort. Perhaps they were primarily engaged in land deals and business. Obviously they were of great practical use to Henry II who bestowed highly personal offices on them.

Some things have come out which to modern ears are bizarre - like one of them being excommunicated for cutting off the tail of a horse or mule that belonged to the Archbishop. But society then was extremely primitive and we ought to remember, when we feel horrified by things that go on in Third World countries today, that all of this is not really all that long ago. I am conscious myself, writing about a period of over 800 years, that I have been here ten percent of that time!

It's probable, but not certain, that during the domination of our manor by the de Brocs, more land must have been cleared because Walter de la Grave had only been allowed two virgates, about sixty acres and at a later date we know there was much more. When that was cleared and by whom and by whose order, we don't know. The last de Broc to own the manor of Grove was Hugh. He joined Edward I in his military campaigns in Wales, Scotland and Gascony, which is probably why he sold the manor. But he messed up the deal and the manor was forfeited to the King who gave it to one of his favourites, Walter Langton.

This is the point where my grandson broke into national history - or rather the records did. They showed that Walter Langton was in possession of the manor by 1307. He was Bishop of Lichfield and Coventry. After he died in 1321 a detailed record was made of his land here, no less than 300 cleared acres of arable land and meadows, plus half a mill, presumably on the River Chess, and several other enclosures. His Inquest Post Mortem which is a list of assets and leases at death, is held in the Public Record Office and is reproduced in Figure 10.

The fact that Walter Langton had 300 acres of arable implies plenty of labour. To cultivate 300 acres with the tools then available, even if it was left fallow every other year, would require a lot of people. Where did they live? There must have been a good number of little wooden houses somewhere around the property, unless of course Whelpley Hill and Ashley Green were already developed and people walked to work. This was the time of the building of the big flint churches in the Chilterns; they too must have absorbed a lot of labour for picking the stone, as well as for the particularly laborious type of masonry. But, of course, it was before the Black Death, so perhaps there was quite a large population.

Figure 10   Grove in 1322

> EXTRACT FROM INQUEST POST MORTEM OF WALTER LANGTON
> Buckingham. Inq. 18 March, 15 Edward II[4]
>
> La Grove. The manor, viz:- a messuage, 180a. arable; 1/2 water-mill and 2a. pasture, held of Robert de Veer, earl of Oxford, in chief, by service of 1/8 knight's fee, and rendering 18s. 4d. yearly, and suit at the said Robert's court of Hegham in Chesham; a sheep fold, stable and 12a. arable, held of Lawrence du Brok in chief in socage, by service of rendering 5s. yearly and suit of court at the manor of Asscheleye; and 120a. arable at Welpeleye, 4a. wood and 2a. meadow, pertaining to the said manor, held of the said Lawrence by service of 1/4 knight's fee, and a pair of spurs price 6d.; 4a. meadow and a moiety of a water-mill, held of Walter de Raan in chief by service of 2d. and a pair of gloves; 24a. arable held of the abbot of Leicester in socage by service of 12d. yearly; 24a. arable held of John le Mareschal by service of 12d. yearly; 42a. arable held of Richard de Browton by homage and scutage when it runs; 17s.11d. rent held in chief of the said Lawrence, service unknown; and 4s. rent, 24a. meadow and a cock and 4 hens, tenure unknown.
> Heir, as above, age unknown.

Walter Langton was far from an ordinary land owner; he had property all over the country. He didn't live at Grove, but probably visited it. He was the King's Treasurer, pretty well the Chancellor of the Exchequer for the whole of

---

4   ie 1322 Cal IPM P.R.O. 1770

England, but he was also thrown into jail when Edward II replaced Edward I. Langton had got himself involved in a lot of shady deals. One was about land between Whelpley and Ashley, two neighbouring villages, which he owned or claimed to own. On some excuse he had imprisoned John Hawkeshead (or Hauksherd) at York (see Figure 11). To get him released John's father Robert had had to promise that John would hand over some land next to Grove and had had to give a guarantee of £200 that John would do so. The guarantee was secured on the land in question. John did hand over the land but Langton tried to get the £200 as well and got an action brought against Robert claiming it as a debt. The case dragged on for ages but the court found in Robert's favour. Langton must have been disappointed!

It is intriguing that Walter Langton was tried in York for an alleged misdemeanour and then later again in Chester and one can imagine the extreme difficulty in getting witnesses from Buckinghamshire to York or Chester. Still the only good straight roads would have been the Roman roads and even on them with horses, it would have taken several days to get there. In the trial it is reported that witnesses didn't turn up and it had to be adjourned. Law must have been a cumbersome business, a very cumbersome business.

Langton's opponent in the case I have quoted - Robert de Haukeserd - where did he come from? Was he simply a neighbour or, like Langton, did he have property all over the country? We have not found much out. If he was a neighbour, was he across the border into Hertfordshire and was the county boundary itself in dispute? He probably was local because he is a witness to a lot of documents which I have seen. But no evidence as to where he lived or what property he held has turned up. He could have lived over the border in Hertfordshire but a brief investigation has shown no trace of him there. In any case it seems unlikely he would have witnessed documents relating to Bucks to such an extent. My own guess is that he lived at the Thorn at Ashley Green. That is a property for which we have found mentions in the 14th century and again in the 15th century. The property in dispute was at least partly the land between Grove and the Thorn. The Thorn must have been substantial because John atte Thorne was the coroner for the area. Nonetheless he was a bad sort. Buckinghamshire Inquests and Indictments 412 notes that: 'Likewise that on Sunday 19 November 1385 the said John (atte Thorne) made an attack on William Puttyhame, a tenant of the Countess of Oxford, at Chesham in a place called Leghe, by force of arms, and there beat, wounded and ill-treated him, against the peace. And that he is a habitual disturber of the peace, by day as well as by night.'

Figure 11   Walter Langton Tries to Get £200[5]

"The sheriff was directed that by fit men (etc) he should make known to Robert of Hawkeshead, or to his heirs or the tenants of his land and tenements if he were dead, that he should be here in the presence of the barons (etc) on a certain day namely a fortnight from Michaelmas (29th of September), to show cause (etc) why £200 which the said Robert had acknowledged before the mayor of the city of York and the clerks appointed to receive acknowledgements of debt in that city, in the 32nd year of the reign of the Lord Edward King of England (6th of May 1304) (i), father of the present King, that he owed to Walter of Langton, bishop of Coventry and Lichfield, lately Treasurer of England, but had failed to pay at the due date, as the said mayor and clerks lately notified to the said barons at the Kings command, should not be levied from the lands and tenements which were his in the aforesaid year, if (etc).

And then came the said Robert by forewarning (etc) and he said that the aforesaid debt ought to be levied from his lands and chattels (etc) because he said that John of Hawkeshead, son of the said Robert, was previously arrested by the adherents of the said bishop, on account of certain offences which he was alleged by the said bishop to have committed, and was imprisoned at York while the king's court was there, until at length the said Robert agreed and made a final concord with the said bishop, that the said John would grant to the said bishop certain lands and tenements which the said John held next to the said bishop's manor of La Grave, in return for this his deliverance (etc).

And on account of the security which the said John, when he was released from prison, gave to the said bishop concerning the lands and tenements aforesaid, the same Robert bound himself to the same bishop for the aforesaid £200 by the statute (etc).

Whence he said that the said John, when he was released from prison, put the said bishop in possession of the lands and tenements according to the said agreement, by which enfeoffment the said bishop was seised of these lands and tenements when the King took the bishop's lands and tenements into his hands. And he asked for judgement (etc).

A day was given him, a fortnight from St. Hilary's day (13th of January). At which time he came and had an adjournment until a fortnight from Easter. At which time he did not come. Therefore a distress was levied on the lands (etc). And that the outgoings (etc). So (etc) a hearing of his judgement a fortnight from St. John the Baptist's day (24th of June ii). At which time the aforesaid Robert came and was allowed a further adjournment to a fortnight from Michaelmas, maintaining the status quo, and further from day to day until William de Beresford should be at liberty to attend. Afterwards on the 15th of December in the third year the said Robert appeared by his attorney, and the treasurer and barons viewed and examined the aforesaid proceedings, the said William sitting with them, and it was testified that the said bishop seised of the lands of the said John next to La Grave on the said occasion, through enfeoffment by the said John, and that this land as well as other lands of the said bishop were taken into the hands of the King (etc).

Whence they agreed that the moneys due by virtue of the said undertaking under the said agreement were not lawfully due, so that the aforesaid demand was at present to be forborne until the king wished to decide otherwise (etc).

NB: Dates in brackets refer to the actual Saints days, as in current practice, except for:
(i) This date was footnoted in the Latin extract and was credited to Exch. Writs 3.
(ii) This refers to St. John the Baptist's official birthday, and not to his martyrdom, which is designated as the 29th of August.

---

5   Trans Dr A. Baines from Camden Soc. 4th SCT. No 6 RHS 1969.

Maybe local people were uncomfortable with Walter Langton, a national figure with great power and therefore arousing jealousy and anger of all sorts, and really nothing whatever to do with the neighbourhood. The King's treasurer from the previous reign would still have had friends in high places and could probably get away with things. He was indeed engaged in land transactions in many parts of the country and cannot really have had much time to spend in his diocese of Coventry and Lichfield.

So far as we have gone, the de Brocs seem to have completely disappeared from Grove. Hugh's son Lawrence may have retained rights over some adjacent land for a while but after a relatively short period, there is no further mention of them. Walter de Langton's heir was a minor so his mother as his "best friend" acted for him. She plainly had some difficulties because the King had to order John Wakewyn, a former tenant "not to intermeddle further" with the affairs of Grove. After that, Grove was held briefly by John de Warenne, Earl of Surrey. He held other local land, including nearby Blackwell Hall. Then all sorts of other family names as owners appear, but none of particular interest until in the middle of the 14th century, when the Cheneys or (to give them their more modern spelling) Cheynes, arrived on the scene. At this point our research more or less collided with the research being done by Anne and Roy Paton, who I met through the Buckinghamshire Record Society, into the family of Cheyne. The Cheynes dominated this area for quite a long while, and became related by marriage to the Russells, who became and remain to this day, Dukes of Bedford.

The Cheynes were such an interesting and active family that they have a chapter all to themselves later in this book. The first Cheyne connected with Grove seems to have been Thomas, Shield Bearer to Edward III and Constable of Windsor Castle. He certainly owned the manor by 1362. When he died the estate passed to William Cheyne who was probably his brother. William was succeeded by his son Roger and then began one of the most colourful episodes in Grove's history because Roger got involved with Lollardy and he and his sons had a spell in the Tower. Subsequently after their father's death, the sons got a fearsome reputation locally for banditry and it took another spell in the Tower to cool them off and set them back on course as respectable citizens. The wording of the commission used to bring them to heel can be read in Figure 13.

The Cheyne involvement with Lollardy illustrated some of the factors that run right through the history of the Cheynes from when they are first mentioned in connection with Grove to the end of their ownership more than two hundred years later. They had a tremendous record in clearing and organising agricultural land, opening up large areas of Bucks. They also had a prodigious talent for making money and were not afraid to defy the establishment. Other Cheynes supported the Lollards in fact one of them spent time in the Tower for appointing a Lollard vicar. So they were people of courage and tremendous enterprise.

Figure 12 Left: Thomas Cheyne d.1368, Shield Bearer to Edward III, the first Cheyne to own Grove
Right: William Cheyne d.1375 the second Cheyne owner of Grove. Both brasses in Drayton Beauchamp Parish Church

Land adjacent to our manor was Cheyne enclosures. The next door farm, now known as Moore's Farm, formerly as Mose Grove, is the land charged to the Cheyne Trust in Chesham, which was established in 1577 by arrangement with one of the last Cheynes to own Grove. There is more evidence of Cheyne enclosures, but no dates as to when they were done. Sheep bells (of a later period) associated with the Cheyne family have been found on the land and they spread from Grove to Chesham Bois and to Chenies village. As an indication of the farming lifestyle in this area just before the Reformation and also of typical farm stock and equipment of the time I reproduce the will of a Marion Morden of Ashley Green as Figure 14.

Figure 13 **Cheynes in the Tower**

> THE ARREST OF JOHN AND THOMAS CHEYNE AND THEIR RELEASE FROM THE TOWER[6]
>
> 6 July 1430   "Commission of Oyer & Terminer to William Babington knight (and others) on complaint by many of the King's lieges of the counties of Hertford and Buckingham made to the Council that John Cheyne of Drayton Co: Bucks: 'chivaler', Thomas Cheyne of Chesham Co: Bucks: esquire, John Watkyns of Stokehamond Co: Bucks: 'gentilman' and Hugh Byllyngdon of Billingdon Co: Bedford 'gentilman' and their accomplices, ministers and servants, have been inflicting divers opressions, extortions (&c.) on divers persons. Some they have with strong hand driven from their own land, some they have beaten, imprisoned and tortured in prison refusing to release them until they have made fine at the will of their oppressors. The houses of others have been broken with armed power, their goods & chattels taken and borne off ... and if they offered to complain they were threatened until they dared not go about their business for fear of death."
>
> 19 June 1431 "Commission to Thomas Sakevyle knight, John Barton the younger and the Sheriff and Escheator of the county of Buckingham to arrest John Cheyne, knight, and bring him before the King and Council. Also the Sheriff and Escheator and the said William (sic) or two of them are to seize the said John Cheyne's manors of Grove and Drayton, all the books, rolls, schedules, bills and suspicious memoranda found therein, and to certify the King in Council of the number and nature of his arms and books &c, aforesaid."
>
> 4 August 1431   "To the Constable of the Tower of London or his lieutenant. Order to suffer Thomas Cheyne esquire, whom by the advice of the Council the King for particular causes lately committed to the Constable's custody, to go free. Like writ in favour of John Cheyne knight."

    One of the 'bandit brothers' Sir John Cheyne, acquired the manor of Chenies in addition to Drayton Beauchamp (near Tring) and Grove, both of which he had inherited from his father Roger. When Sir John's widow died Chenies went to her niece Anne Philip whose grand-daughter married John, Earl of Bedford and thus initiated the link between the manor of Chenies and the Bedford family so many of whom now lie at rest in their private chapel there.

---

6   Calendar of Patent Rolls 1429-36 pp75 and 153 and the writ for release from Calendar of Close Rolls 1429-35 p89. All at the P.R.O. and extracted in this form by Cdr Smith.

Figure 14   A Farmer's Lifestyle in the Time of Henry VIII

THE WILL OF MARION MORDEN[7]

In dei nomine Amen the xiij day of May in the yere of Our Lord God mccccxxj [13 May 1521] I **Marion Morden** of Assheley Grene in the paryssh of Chessham Leiceter Lincoln dioc' hole of mynd and in good memory beyng doth make and orden my present testament and last will in this maner.

First I bequeth my sowle to God Father Allmyghty and to Our blissid Lady seynt Mary and to all the seynts in heuyn and my body to [be] burid in the church yard of blissid Mary of Chessham next the sepulcur of my husband.

Item I bequeth for my mortuary as the vse and custome his.
Item I bequeth to the mother church of Lyncoln iiij d.
Item I bequeth to the reparation of Our Lady chapell in Chessham xij d.
Item I bequeth to all the lightes in the church of Chessham aforsaid a good shepe.
Item I bequeth to the torchis in the same church vj d.
Item I bequeth to Marion Mordon the doughter of Herry Morden a yong ewe shepe.
Item to Marion Butterfeld a pugge ewe shepe.
Item to Christofer Ouerstrete a yong ewe shepe.
Item to William Putnam the son of John Putnam of Hawryge iij s. iiij d.
Item to Richard Leche a lambe.
Item to Marion Wedon an ewe shepe of the best and oon of my best platers and on shete.
Item to Thomas Wedon a lambe and a salt celler.
Item to Herry Wedon a lambe and on of my second best candilstikkes.
Item to Marion Wedon a lambe and on my best platters.
Item to John Wedon the yonger a lambe.
Item to John Leche on lambe.
Item to Robert Shorte a lambe.
Item to Joan Lote and to Richarad here son on good shepe betwen them bothe.
Item to Isabell Wedon a lambe and a shepe.
Item to Isabell Asshford an handyll panne and on lambe when she ys cum to here full age.
Item the residewe of my goods moveable and unmoveable after my dettes be paid and my funeral expenses don and this my present testament fullfilled I gyve and bequeth to Joan my doughter and to here childern and also I orden and make Robert Wedon and Thomas Harding of Chesham myn executours they to dispose it for the helthe of my woule and my frendes sowles.
Item I make Robert Hutton of Chesham superuisour of this my last weill.

Thies being present Master Christofer Rudde curate and vicar, sir Richard Bolde, Thomas Bolde, Thomas Sawnders, Nicholas Lot Wt other mo.

Dat' die et anno domini predictis.

Probatum fuit presens testamentum coram nobis Thoma Jakeman in legibus baccallario commissario et officiali archidiaconatus Buck' xvj die Septembris anno domini millesimo quingentesimo xxj [16 September 1521]. Commissiaque est administracio omnium bonorum ipsius defuncte executoribus in eadem testamente nominatis admissis et iuratis saluo jure cuiuscum que. Dat' die et anno domini predictis.

---

[7] BRS Vol 19 - 402

This link with the Bedfords in a sense continues the Cheyne characteristics of independence and enterprise. In the 18th and 19th century the Dukes of Bedford supported non-conformity as well as the established church. There are Bedford chapels all over the place sponsored or provided by Dukes or Duchesses of Bedford. This behaviour has carried on right into the present century when the Russells have at times dissociated themselves from the establishment. But also of course in the 17th and 18th century they had been responsible for drainage of a great part of Lincolnshire: the main river, artificial river or artificial diversion of existing rivers draining a large part of the fens known as the Bedford Level. This was financed by the Duke of Bedford and carried out by Dutch engineers employed by him. And in spite of their eccentricity and their non-conformity at times, or at least support of non-conformity, they remain an extremely rich and successful family.

During the 16th century a member of the Cheyne family who probably remained a Catholic, came into possession of the manor of Grove and he sold most of it in 1578 to Thomas Southen or Southam and pretty well the rest of it to John Partridge. From then on, the history is largely one of a breaking-up of the unit for the time being. As described earlier, John Partridge gave a field away to his daughter when she got married to Edmund Wethered in Ashley Green and the document describes the fields around it all being under separate ownerships. Partridge must have been the owner in order to be able to convey it. The effect of all this was that the land going with Grove itself by 1660 was just 104 acres. A schedule of the property of the Bunn family made thirty years later, is shown as Figure 15.

A SURVEY OF GROVE PARK IN YE PARISH OF CHESHAM FOR M. HENRY BUNN, MARCH 17, 1690/1

	Ac	R	P.
Further Grove Field	9	1	25
Middle Grove Field	5	2	17
Hither Grove Field	7	0	14
Six Acres Close	7	1	35
Chalkdell Close	5	1	36
Grove Field	8	1	13
Pond Field	9	1	2
New Lands	12	2	7
The Wood	4	1	18
Stock Piece	6	3	6
New Close	4	0	34
Spring Close	2	2	5
Wood Close	5	3	5
The Meade	7	0	28
The House, orchards, banks & moats	8	1	16
	104	1	5

Done by Tho. Pegsworth

Source: Lowndes Papers D/LO/4/2

Figure 15   Grove in the Time of William III

This indicates that farming in the Chilterns was still in small units from when the original manors were broken up and before the big estates were assembled in the late 17th and early 18th century of course the 17th and 18th centuries were periods of rapid agricultural development - new methods coming from the continent, new buildings being built, successful farmers taking over the land of less successful farmers, and in the end as far as Grove was concerned, a big estate being built up again.

The process of once again becoming part of a large land holding happened to Grove with its purchase by William Lowndes. William Lowndes like his predecessor Walter Langton 400 years before, was at the centre of the country's finances, namely Secretary to the Treasury. He began to build up an estate in the Chesham area in 1687 and in 1692 he bought Grove. One field had been mortgaged by its owner to Benjamin Vaughan who appears to have foreclosed and passed it on to Mr. Lowndes. There is also a document that shows the Weathered family discharging liabilities on land they had held for over a hundred years before selling it to William Lowndes.

Figure 16   Another 17th Century Land Deal

October 1st, 1694
Received of John Weatheredd, Yeoman of the Parish of Chesham, the sum of Fifteen pounds of lawful English money - being the residue of the sum of Fourscore pounds which was the Dowry and portion of Elizabeth Bampton my wife - given and Bequeathed to her by her Father, John Weatheredd the Elder deceased As by his last will and testament may appear which said sum of fourscore pounds I do by these presents Acknowledge and declare that I have received and do discharge the said John Weatheredd from the same his Heirs and .... - for ever and from every part and parcel thereof I say wi' in full of all Debts .... and demands from the Beginning of the world to this day the said sum of fourscore pounds

By me   Timothy Bampton
                                the marke of Elizabeth X Bampton
Witnesses -
Thos: Barritt
Elizabeth Wetheredd
    her X Marke
            Examined with the original receipt
                    By me   Tho Holloway Marshall

Gradually Grove itself was returning to almost its medieval dimensions. Activity here throughout the 18th century would be much the same as on the other farms in the Chilterns, same methods, same products, same tenancy, sending stuff into London and bringing down the refuse from London. This all went on right into the 20th century. But before we get there, there are things about the 18th and 19th centuries at Grove which require explanation.

In the first records of 18th century transactions and in later documents including the first ordnance survey map, there is mention of a chapel at The Grove. It indeed is still shown on the map. No mention prior to that, so why was it called a chapel? In the 18th century minutes of the Chesham Baptists, the following minute appears.

Figure 17   A Dispute among Baptists

> "...Sister Widmer was blamed that when she let her farm she did not oblige John Casson to let Bro. Honor remain unmolested as her tenant till Michaelmas that he might take the profit of the summer half-year arising from his garden. She said she was sorry it so happened, that she did not know and consider better, it being the custom at Chesham in respect of tenements to give on either side but a quarter's warning.
>
> But as Sister Widmer as soon as convinced of her error promised before Bro. Sexton, Bro. Sale, and Bro. ....at the Grove house even when Bro. Honor yet dwelt in it to indemnify him if John Casson injured him, she was judged not deserving of a sharp reproof.
>
> Bro. Honor was judged worthy of and accordingly greatly blamed for railing against and reproaching Sister Widmer with such bitterness of spirit as he hath done, who at the first did not receive it as becomes a Christian, but at length by means of the reproof and advice given him by friends present and God's blessing thereon he appeared to be of a better spirit and said he was sorry he had spoke a word against her."

This is an interesting insight into the area at that time when the vast majority of farmers in this part of the Chilterns were Baptists, living to a very rigid standard of behaviour. This record of the case of Mrs. Widmer suggests that she may have been a tenant of the Lowndes family with power to sub-let. The dispute concerned who should have the vegetables when the lease ran out in September. Don't take it to the County Court, take it to the Elders of the Baptist Chapel who decided "He who sows, shall reap" - therefore the gardener was right. Mrs. Widmer could easily have been the widow of a Jonathan Widmer who was the Baptist Minister in Chesham. Certainly she was the widow of a well-known Baptist family, so isn't it very probable that at that time the house was used as a chapel by the local Baptist community? The Chiltern countryside was overwhelmingly Baptist. The nearby tiny hamlet of Whelpley Hill had a Baptist chapel with an average congregation of 35, according to the religious census of 1851 when there were probably not more than 60 or 70 people living there and every other village shows the same picture.

The Baptist minutes also suggest that our neighbours at the Thorne had not become completely respectable, even after several hundred years, at least by Buckinghamshire Baptists' standards which are rather exacting. There is a record in the minutes of Mr.Tomalin of the Thorne being thrown out of the Chapel for bad behaviour, bad language etc!

About one hundred years or so later, three local land-owners were to build Church of England churches in the villages, I think to wean their tenants from non-conformity. Lord Chesham built St. Georges, at Tylers Hill, Ley Hill; Mr. Smith Dorrien St. John's at Ashley Green; and Mr. Constable Curtiss a church at Whelpley Hill. I think it's probable that this was the time our building was turned into a barn when it was no longer needed as a chapel. There had already been another house built on the farm adjacent to the farm buildings, separate to the one Mrs. Widmer was occupying.

In 1798 Arthur Young, surveying the area along the Bucks/Herts border, remarked upon the number of orchards, saying: "The smaller the farm, the bigger the orchard". Of course orchards were a way of increasing the cash return from small farms. It was a big fruit growing area for a while.

There is an interesting entry in the Posse Comitatus of 1798, a call-up register for a possible French invasion. Part of the entry for the Burnham Hundred of Buckinghamshire is shown below.

Figure 18   Horsepower at Grove

Buckinghamshire to wit Hundred of Burnham. A register of the Names of the Persons within the said Hundred who keep Draught Horses, Waggons or Carts of Burthen, the Numbers thereof by them respectively kept and of the Persons Occupying any Wind or Water Corn Mill with the Average Weekly Quantity of Corn that can be Ground thereat as returned by the Petty Constables within the said Hundred in pursuance of a precept from John Penn Esq, High Sheriff of the said County bearing date the 16th Day of February, 1798. For the better ascertaining the Civil power of the said County.

.....
Ashley Green   John Barnes   6 Horses   2 Waggons   2 Carts
.....

This John Barnes was tenant of Grove. He had pretty well exactly the number of horses and wagons and carts that Benny Wingrove (the tenant in 1918) had, proving that the output of the farm had not varied very much for 120 years.

The Lowndes family held Grove for two hundred and thirty years. They enlarged the farm area by taking over Sales Farm next door and other property around. One of them got into debt and his father put the property into the hands of trustees to avoid it being gambled away. One of William Lowndes grandsons lost his wife soon after their marriage. He never remarried but he had two children by a Mrs Harrington. He made very substantial provision for her and the children. A similar a charge was on the property when my father bought it in 1919, not relating to the then Squire Lowndes but to his cousin from whom he had inherited.

Much of our information we have got from property deals of one sort or another. Although farming methods were changing, and changing fast, and people were drifting from the countryside into the towns there was a period of stability during the 19th century. The squires like the Lowndes remained largely in control, right up to the time (just before the First World War) when commuters started moving in from other places.

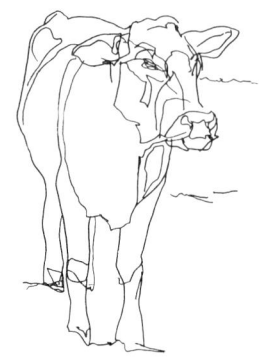

The dispersal of the Lowndes estate commenced with the sale of Grove Farm to my father and continued throughout the 1920's. I look on my father as the first of the commuters. He wasn't a farmer but he wanted to farm. He travelled backwards and forwards to London, he did what is now called 'gentrify' his farm house and started to farm. He would have made a good farmer, he recorded so many sensible ideas in his papers, but of course a considerable slump in farming had started by the beginning of the 20th century. It was arrested very briefly by the first world war which caused more interest in output, but then there was a steady decline right until the second world war.

This had a profound effect on the ownership of the countryside. The landlords who already, throughout the previous century, had had more and more of their income and capital involved in industrial and city projects, turned their back on the countryside. Locally in particular as in most of the country, many many estates were broken up and sold in the early twenties. They were often sold as individual farms to the tenants who didn't look as far ahead as their landlords and didn't realise the depths to which the slump would effect them. So during this period they sometimes kept themselves going selling hedgerow trees and altering the look of the countryside, selling odd plots of land where they could to would-be commuters, thereby starting the ribbon development which has had so much effect on all the counties around London.

It is difficult to talk about the last hundred years because too much is recorded! It is too close for one to understand what are the really important things. So just as at the beginning of our story we miss a century through things not being recorded, at the end we have a difficult century because everything is recorded and we don't know what is important. But I did do my best with my book Seventy Summers, to fill that gap, so I personally won't try to do it again. It is illuminating to think one has been here for nearly 10% of a thousand years – well 8.5% anyway.

Of course things don't happen now as they did at the time of my predecessors. I haven't gone around stealing my neighbours' land like Walter Langton, nor making forays into their houses as John and Thomas Cheyne did, robbing them. Fortunately these things have been not open to my neighbours to do to me either! At least in this respect we have moved from a 'wild west' situation to a modern, orderly and civilised society.

Epilogue

The whole of my life I've been thinking about the place where I live, listening to old men's tales, titbits of information from various sources and doing a bit of investigation of historical documents. I had a feeling that somewhere I should find the dates of enclosure of all the lands, prove or disprove my own theories, think about what the farming practices must have been to achieve those clearances and to maintain them. On most of those subjects I have still got nothing, but I have found so much more that is worth recording about this Chiltern farm – who owned it, who lived here and what they did, good or evil.

Of course it is inevitable if you start any sort of historical research, especially with limited resources, that you finish up realising your own ignorance more than anything else. I still want to know when the land was enclosed and if possible by whom and which field was enclosed first and which last. I can only guess at this by the nature of the enclosure. Who built the earliest part of the house and who dug the moat? We still haven't the slightest idea. We've got a list of possible people who might have built the house, because we have a list of ownership from 1128 but no clues about who dug the moat – it was there in 1128, almost certainly. There are small things, like was Walter de la Grave a Norman or a Saxon, it was not long after the conquest that he was given this grant. He may have been a sort of quisling Saxon, or he may have been a Norman; I suspect the former but it is only a suspicion, I don't know. Who was Robert Hauksherd (or Hawkeshead) whose dispute with Walter Langton was tried by the Baron's Court? No word of him in any Bucks record that we have seen. We have to search every county record in England maybe to find him, and then maybe we wouldn't. Maybe he was just an ordinary man farming in this area, owning a freehold, maybe the progenitor of a family now called Hawkes; who knows and we can't find out. But reading this book, somebody may write and tell me they know all about it, they have seen it in the records of some other county.

Sitting on the moat bank as a little boy, I had dreamed of robber barons. Walter Langton could be described as a sleazy bishop with his land deals. Thomas Cheyne was not a baron, not a robber baron, but something near it, a robber knight may be? Arrested by the King's men from London for extracting money under torture from his neighbours in Bucks and Herts, he too pretty well got away with it. The Cheyne family continued in their ownership and occupation of Grove as a small manor with the additional land Langton, and no doubt others had owned, right up until after the dissolution of the monasteries. Then in 1578 Thomas Southen and John Partridge came on the scene. Was the latter a member of the family named Partridge who looked after some of the land in this area on behalf of the Bishop of Lincoln? It is quite possible but we simply don't know.

I have been intrigued by the fact that so many property deals begin with the property having been owned by a woman. So much of Chesham - Elgiva, so much of Berkhamsted - somebody called Edith; to the extent that the men in possession at the time of the Conquest were known as 'Edith's men' or one of 'Edith's men'. Women must have been considerable property owners in Saxon times and that must be worth a study. In Norman times women didn't seem to have much in the way of property rights.

Right through the whole of this story there are clues to other things one would like to investigate if it was possible.

For instance we could get a geophysical survey done of the whole site to see what other buildings may have been here. We could perhaps have radiocarbon dating of the half-burnt ash around the pieces of Belgic pottery found in one corner of the moat, which might date part of the moat. We could have radiocarbon dating of two bits of timber in the most ancient part of the house, which were too small to date by dendro-chronology. Lots more wants doing; who knows, somebody may do it one day.

But in the meantime we have done well to get together as much of the story as we have. Following my first researches, two years ago my grandson Thor Harman spent the whole of one vacation 'digging up' things about Grove. He found a lot – even though they were not things I was initially looking for! Then I met up with Roy and Anne Paton who contributed information about the Cheyne family. Jennifer Moss has given me a lot of material about Grove from the end of the 16th to the beginning of the 20th century. Dr Arnold Baines has encouraged my research and provided a picture of the earliest days of our district for the first hundred years of this tale.

These people have contributed the pages that follow – the 'chapter and verse', the intriguing detail underlying the story I have told of a thousand years on this Chiltern farm.

What the Records Tell Us About Grove

1   From Pre-history to the 11th Century
by Dr Arnold Baines

It seems likely that Grove Farm, Ashley Green or The Grove, as it has been called for most of its history, was already in being before the year 1000, though no written record has survived to confirm this. A thousand years earlier still, there had been a defended settlement at Whelpley Hill, represented until Victorian times by Round Field inside Banks Wood, rather like a smaller version of Cholesbury. Then the wood was felled and the banks ploughed out, but enough of them still remain for the site to be scheduled as an ancient monument, and to confirm that this north-eastern quarter of Great Chesham had been settled in the pre-Roman Iron Age, perhaps as a venture into new territory.

The Romans did not like such tribal hill-forts, and soon relocated the native British population onto villa estates centred on riverside sites such as Latimer in the Chess valley and Northchurch on the Bulbourne. During the Dark Age of warfare and pestilence which followed the end of Roman and sub-Roman rule in the 5th century, the Chiltern plateau must, in any case, have reverted to scrub on its way back to high forest, especially where the chalk is covered by clay-with-flints rather than sand or gravel. Verulam ceased to function as the provincial capital; urban life there collapsed, and although Christian worship and works of healing were maintained at St. Alban's shrine, pilgrims from the Christian west-country could no longer reach it.

In the central Chilterns, the surviving Britons became an impoverished and wandering folk, without ordered government, without coinage or pottery, living a precarious life dominated by their search for food and by fear of their heathen neighbours. The Anglo-Saxon newcomers could help themselves to as much woodland and rough grazing as they needed, or thought they might need. Dense woods, and infertile soil where the Chiltern dip-slope was not wooded, did not invite initiatives by humble folk, but there were some enterprising leaders who secured ready-made estates for themselves and farmlands for their companions, with British serfs to work on them until a new peasantry could move in. The natives were assimilated by intermarriage, by the replacement of their Primitive Welsh language by Old English, and soon by sharing the Christian faith. In any event the Britons, locally called Cumbre 'fellow-countrymen', would still have been needed on the demesne[8] or as swineherds in the woods.

---

8   Land on a manor reserved for the Lord's own use

Such a colonising movement from Middlesex was probably the origin of the great estate of Chesham, occupying some 20 square miles, centred on the water meadows where three streams unite to form the river Chess. At the turn of the millennium this was still assessed for taxation and military service at 15 hides, which should have represented about 1800 acres under cultivation, barely one-seventh of its area. This may have been fair enough when the assessment was made, but its continuance looks like a deliberate concession, perhaps at the instance of the Lady Elgiva in the mid-10th century, when settlement was still hazardous enough to need positive encouragement.

Figure 19   North side of the moat at Grove looking west. Was this contemporary with Bygrave 973AD?

Resettlement did not take the form of compact villages, as in the Vale of Aylesbury, but rather of dispersed farmsteads, located where surface water could be retained in ponds on the impermeable clays. Grove may have been among the first of these pioneer farms; it was the only one in the neighbourhood which became a manor, though it remained formally subordinate throughout the Middle Ages to the principal manor of Chesham Higham.

A thousand years ago Grove Farm was probably already moated, and not merely as a status symbol. Its double moat has a parallel at Bygrave in

Hertfordshire, where at least one of the moats was already there in 973, when the name is first recorded as *Bygrafan* 'by the entrenchment' or 'entrenchments', as the word can be singular or plural. Grove was probably named from its location in the woods rather than from its earthworks, but in both places the moats, probably reinforced by stockades, would have secured sheep and cattle by night in dangerous times. As arable cultivation was extended, the moats would still have served to pen the livestock, even in more peaceful years. At Bygrave there appears to have been a larger and later enclosure, corresponding to the two virgates (60 acres) at Grove whose outline is still visible. Ten centuries ago the surrounding area was still ancient woodland, not yet felled or burnt. The word for a clearing, *leah* in Old English, is found locally in Ashley Green, Lye Green and Ley Hill, and it occurs not far away as The Lee. In Nashleigh, the old pronunciation Nashleeth suggests a different word, *hlith* 'hillside'.

Each of the scattered farms would have been the home of an extended family, probably working with the help of two or three bondsmen and perhaps also of some penal slaves. The Saxons did not like prisons and preferred to make offenders pay their debt to society by penal servitude on the land. Elgiva used some on her upland hamlets around Risborough, and liberated them by her will, with King Edgar's consent.

Great Chesham was separated from the post-Roman region called Hemel by the dry valley running up from Flaunden Bottom all the way to its head at Whelpley Hill. This was probably a frontier which had long since been agreed by East Saxons and Middle Saxons, and it has divided Herts from Bucks since these counties were established in the 10th century. Whelpley Hill is the only settlement between Grove Farm and this county boundary which could be called a hamlet, but it did not qualify as one of the eight hamlets of Great Chesham. Instead it was intricately divided between two of these: Ashley Green (which included Grove, Moor's and Whelpley Hill Farms) and (surprisingly) Latimer, which included Heming's and Spencer's Farms, as well as a detached area comprising Bush Wood and six adjoining fields. Sale's Farm was on the hamlet boundary.

Whelpley is 'whelp's clearing', where the young animals played, but the original settlement by a group from Latimer may well have been at the Whelpley Fields south of the Bourne Gutter, where there are cultivation terraces on the slope of Mount's Hill, like the Balks in the Town Field of Chesham. The adjoining higher ground, called Great and Little Furlongs, was also cultivated in the strips, locally called slipes, which characterise an open common field; the tithe map shows that some of these remained in different ownership until the 1840's. The midstream of the Bourne Gutter was taken as the county boundary, no doubt by agreement, but it looks as if there was a scramble to claim the woodlands called Great Wood or Dark Grove, extending almost to Bourne End. This remote corner of Great Chesham, and therefore of the Chiltern Hundreds, remained part of Buckinghamshire until 1991, when it was ceded to Dacorum, the 'Danish' district of Hertfordshire.

Ten centuries before, when the water-table was higher, the Bourne Gutter would have risen further up Hockeridge Bottom, providing a reliable source of water. Well Field, upstream from Bottom Mead, may define one stage in its retreat; 'well' means spring or source. One suspects that what happened was that Elgiva in the 10th century, or Queen Edith or Brihtric in the eleventh, settled a group of freedmen here, maybe with one or two oxen apiece, as a ploughteam for their allotted acres. This, however was exceptional; most farms were held 'in severalty' ie. privately by one person.

The names of fields often indicate that they had once been woodland. Names such as Reddings or Reading (meaning 'ridding'), Grove Field, Wood Field, The Breach, New Ground and New Lands all recall clearance at different periods. Initially, however, clearance may simply have extended the area of rough pasture. In this neighbourhood, 'moor' means uncultivated upland, not riverside marshes such as Chesham Moor and Frogmoor. There was plenty of such moorland awaiting the plough. Meanwhile, bracken as well as mast could support pigs, and the moordriver was a traditional officer in each hamlet. Intermediate stages between ancient woodland and arable are evidenced by such names as Briary Close, Thorne, Great and Little Bushy Fields and especially by the 'moor' names such a Rushmoor, Felmoor and Deldermoor around Grove Farm, and Overmoor on the Bovingdon boundary. Moor's Farm however, used to be Mose Farm or The Mose.

By 1000 AD, there would have been a regular rotation of crops and fallow, settled communally for the limited area of common field but individually on the separate farms. Some fields seem to have been assigned to particular crops - there are Hither and Further Flax Fields and a Rye Field nearby - corresponding names are found in 10th century surveys elsewhere. Incidentally, the climate was rather warmer than at present and rabbits had not yet arrived.

The only mills were on the rivers; the windmill had not yet reached England and grain from Grove Farm and its neighbours would have had to be ground at Chesham at Lord's Mill, then recently established by diverting the Chess at Waterside. Previously hand-querns were used.

Horse-ploughing had not yet replaced the traditional teams of four oxen, and cows were kept mainly to breed replacements for the ploughteam. Horses were surely better adapted to the small fields of the district, as they could plough faster and straighter and could cope better with stony ground, but after his working life the ox, unlike the horse, could provide the household with lean meat. Possibly the use of horses had to await the introduction of legumes, especially the vetch, as fodder crops in the rotation. It was already well known that the Norsemen used horses to draw their ploughs, and it may have been partly through Danish influence that the Chilterns were to become a progressive farming area, leading the way in innovations.

One anonymous writer, apparently the reeve of a major estate somewhere in the Midlands, has left us what seems to be a unique account of the agricultural routine shortly before the Norman Conquest, and this is worth summarising, though he emphasises that practice varied. He says that in May, June and July men harrow, spread manure, set up hurdles, shear the sheep, make good the fences and buildings, cut wood, clear the ground of weeds, make sheep-pens and construct fish-weirs. During the next three months, they reap, mow, set woad with the dibble, thatch and cover the crops, clear out the fields, prepare the sheep-pens and pig-sties and ploughs. During the winter they plough, in frosty weather split timber, prepare orchards, put the cattle in the stalls and the pigs in sties, set up a drying oven on the threshing-floor and provide a hen-roost. In spring they graft, sow beans, make ditches, hew wood to keep out wild deer, set madder, sow flax and woad and plant the vegetable garden. The writer concludes, "I have spoken about what I know; he who knows better, let him say more."

Note by the Editor: Grove is scheduled as an Ancient Monument. Its great ditch, moat and the remains of ramparts are its most visible archaeological features, but as records of the past they are at present uninformative. A fragment of Belgic pottery has been found possibly at original ground level at the north-west corner and some Romano-British pottery sherds have been recovered from the bottom of the moat, but there is, at present, no other evidence from these early periods.

It is not possible to identify precisely which entry in Domesday applies to this site. The entry entitled Grove relates to a property in Cottesloe Hundred near Wing. It is likely that the Chesham Grove is covered in Domesday by the entry for the lands that Hugh de Bolbec was holding that Brihtric, Queen Edith's man, had held in 1066.[9] Subsequently, these became known as the manor of Chesham Higham which included Grove as a sub-manor.

---

9   Domesday Bucks 26.3

The reference to Walter 'de la Grave', in connection with the early grant of two virgates in 1128, may mean that the property was then already noted for its great ditch. It has been suggested that the rectangular characteristics of the earthworks indicate a medieval origin but rectangular enclosures of much earlier date do exist. By the time of the Cheynes in the 15th century Grove was a domestic stronghold. It is possible that the medieval occupants improved an already well-defended site to meet their needs and did not construct the earthworks from scratch. There is no recorded evidence of Grove ever having been a truly military feature. The true date and purpose of the original earthworks currently remain unknown.

2 The 12th and 13th Centuries: the de Brocs

by Roy Paton and Thor Harman

In 1128 Walter 'de la Grave' received a grant of two virgates of land (60 acres).[10] It is very likely that these two virgates were those centred upon Grove and that Walter's description as being 'de la Grave' meant that he was already living by the great ditch or entrenchment.

Walter's family name was probably de Broc. In the 12th century a Walter de Broc and his brother Hunfrey de Hida (connected with Hyde Heath) were issuing and witnessing charters in the Chesham area.[11] The de Brocs owned Hundridge Manor. In the middle of the 12th century (after 1128) we have a reference to a Walter de Broc at Grove.[12] This mid 12th century Walter was married to Maud and their son Robert is said to have been the ancestor of Laurence de Broc who was a lawyer very active in Buckinghamshire from at least 1236 until his death in 1274/5. Laurence certainly did hold Grove.

Robert Halstead, who compiled the genealogies of certain important families in 1685,[13] believed that this Laurence de Broc was directly descended from the Rannulf de Broc who had custody of Archbishop Becket's lands in Kent in 1164-70.[14] Halstead believed this descent to be through Rannulf's son, Robert who he termed 'marshal of England'.[15] Other sources show that this 'Robert, the marshal' was Rannulf's nephew.[16] Whatever the relationship, this Robert was

---

10 BCRO document not identified, see Appendix 1
11 MAC Vol. II pp. 3-7
12 VCH Bucks III p.212
13 R. Halstead Succinct Genealogies pub. 1685
14 F. Barlow Thomas Becket p.126 et seq.
15 Halstead, ibid.
16 Barlow p.301 n55

undoubtedly Rannulf's right hand man and took over the office of Usher of the King's Bedchamber which Rannulf had held.[17] That he was not Rannulf's son is probably confirmed by his not inheriting Rannulf's estates. These were in Surrey and passed to Rannulf's five daughters, the eldest of whom Adelina, married Stephen Thornham (Turnham),[18] who had a little land in Buckinghamshire[19]

Rannulf's direct relationship with Laurence de Broc therefore depends on one of the several Roberts who appear in the family tree of the Grove de Brocs having been Rannulf's nephew. (Figure 20 The de Broc Family) As Rannulf was active in the second half of the 12th century, this can only really be satisfactorily explained if Rannulf was the brother of Walter and Hunfrey, and Robert the 'marshal' was the son of Walter and Maud. This also raises a yet unanswerable question about who was the father of Walter, Hunfrey and Rannulf![20]

Whether or not he was 'Robert, the marshal', Robert the son of Walter and Maud married Emma de Wimberville, a member of an important Norman family. They had several children, some of whom took the name de Wimberville and several the name de Broc.[21] The eldest, Elias de Wimberville was acknowledged by his brother Robert, as his overlord[22] but Elias died and Robert, presumably the next eldest son, inherited his properties. There is evidence that Robert and his sister Matilda de Wimberville may have used Grove around this time.[23]

This Robert had a son Richard who married firstly, Iterie, sister of Hugh de Botte and, secondly, Cecily de Brai. These two marriages throw light on both Grove in Chesham and Grove near Wing. Hugh de Botte arranged that after he died the Wing Grove should pass to his sister Iterie's son, another Robert, in terms that indicated the boy and his father Richard lived at the Chesham Grove.[24] In 1197, Cecily brought a case against Richard's nephew Osbert, in respect of her interests in the property at Wing and a deal was struck involving an exchange of leases between the properties at Wing and at Chesham.[25] Osbert was styled 'de la Grave' and his father Walter, seems to have been known under both names of 'la Grave' and de Broc.

---

17 Cal. IPM. 15 Edward II No. 44
18 Halstead, ibid.
19 VCH Bucks IV pp.289 & 290
20 Barlow, Ibid. p.301 n55 says Rannulf's father was Oin Purcell and that Rannulf had lands in Surrey from him
21 Luffield Priory Charters Vol II p.xlviii
22 MAC Vol II p.9
23 Cal.IPM 3 Edit 1, file 9
24 VCH III p.361
25 Ibid.

Figure 20   **De Broc Family**

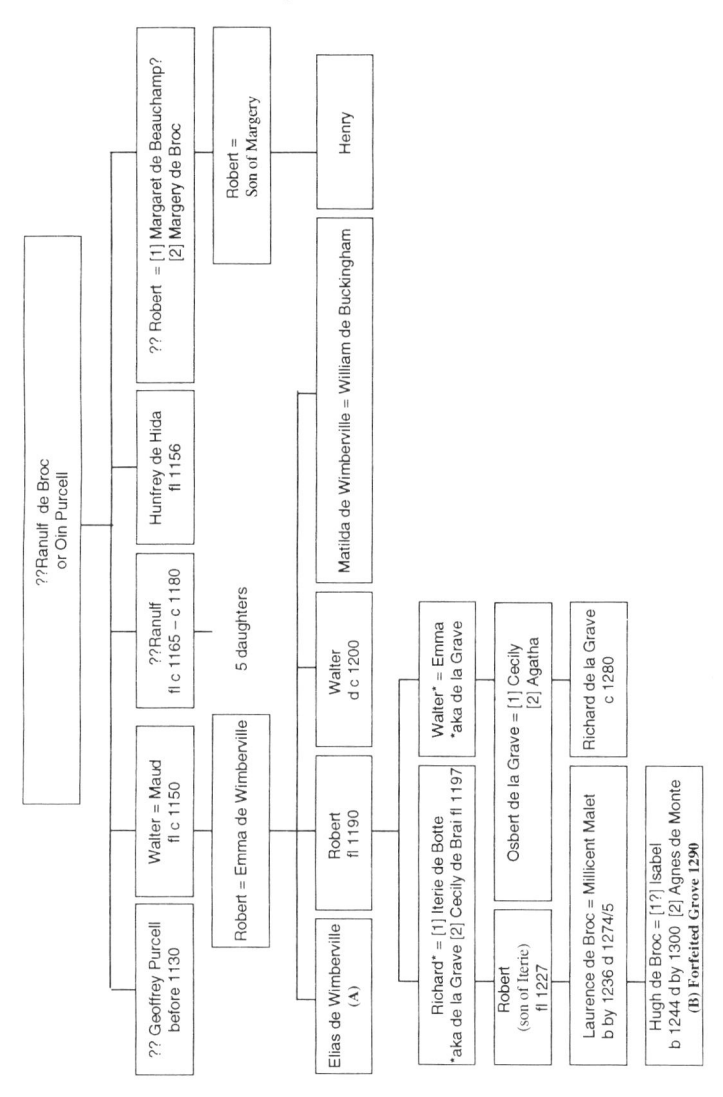

```
                                    ??Ranulf de Broc
                                    or Oin Purcell
         ┌──────────────────┬──────────────────┬──────────────────┐
    Walter = Maud      ??Ranulf         Hunfrey de Hida    ?? Robert = [1] Margaret de Beauchamp?
    fl c 1150          fl c 1165 – c 1180   fl 1156                    [2] Margery de Broc
         │                   │                                              │
??Geoffrey Purcell      5 daughters                                    Robert =
before 1130        Robert = Emma de Wimberville                        Son of Margery
                          │                                                 │
                   Elias de Wimberville                                   Henry
                         (A)
                   Matilda de Wimberville = William de Buckingham
                   
                   Walter
                   d c 1200
                   │
                   Robert
                   fl 1190
                   │
                   Richard* = [1] Iterie de Botte         Walter* = Emma
                   *aka de la Grave [2] Cecily de Brai fl 1197   *aka de la Grave
                   │
                   Robert              Osbert de la Grave = [1] Cecily
                   (son of Iteric)                          [2] Agatha
                   fl 1227
                                       Laurence de Broc = Millicent Malet     Richard de la Grave
                                       b by 1236 d 1274/5                     c 1280
                                       │
                                       Hugh de Broc = [1?] Isabel
                                       b 1244 d by 1300 [2] Agnes de Monte
                                       (B) Forfeited Grove 1290
```

NOTE: All patronyms are de Broc unless otherwise indicated eg. De la Grave, de Wimberville etc.
(A)   This line probably continues as the de Brocs of Hundridge Manor, Chesham
(B)   Connection with Grove ends around this time, Hugh's son Laurence lived elsewhere, probably at Ellesborough
??   Indicates Possible relationships, still being researched

Robert, who had received the Wing property at Hugh de Botte's death, leased the Chesham Grove or part of it to Hugh de Bathon.[26] This deed is dated 1227. Robert later witnessed many documents relating to Missenden Abbey.[27] Most of these documents are dated to the mid-1260's which means they overlap with the period of his son, Laurence de Broc's, greatest activity. Laurence, as has been noted, was an attorney and in 1236 he started a long series of land purchases around Chesham.[28]

Laurence died in 1275[29] and left a son Hugh, as his heir. Hugh was a military man and served the King in wars in Wales, Gascony and Scotland.[30] Perhaps to finance these expeditions, he began to dispose of his estates. In 1286 he alienated Grove for a fee to Roger de Drayton and Robert de Hemel Hempstead.[31] However, he somehow failed to keep his agreement and the manor was forfeit to the King in 1290.[32] Hugh's son, another Laurence, had been fortunate enough to have been given other de Broc lands at Ellesborough a few years earlier. He probably based his family there, the Ellesborough estate eventually passing by marriage to the Mordaunts. Similarly, the de Broc property at Wing was disposed of in 1349 to Sir Neil Loring.[33] Possibly the last act of the de Brocs at Chesham was to farm the land for a while for its new owners in the 1290's. It appears that they retained ownership of some adjacent land until at least the 1320s.[34]

3 The 14th Century: Walter Langton

by Roy Paton, Tony and Thor Harman

By 1300, Edward I had bestowed Grove on Walter de Langton who obtained a grant of free warren there that year.[35] Walter de Langton was the King's Treasurer and right hand man. He had become Bishop of Coventry and Lichfield in 1296.[36] He was accused of devil worship in 1301 and acquitted by a Papal Commission.[37] His position at court and his acquisitiveness made him many enemies and on Edward I's death in 1307 Edward II seized all Langton's

---

26 Bucks Feet of Fines, Vol I p.57 No 27
27 MAC Vol II PP. 293, 298-301
28 Bucks FF Vols I & II
29 VCH III p.210
30 Halstead Ibid.
31 VCH III p.210
32 Cal Close Rolls Ed I
33 VCH III p.361
34 Cal IPM 15 Edward II 44
35 VCH p.211
36 Camden Fourth Series 6 p.1
37 Thomas, K. Religion and the Decline of Magic p.444 n.1

assets and properties including Grove.[38] However, the new King, having become very unpopular himself with his courtiers, fairly rapidly changed his mind and Langton's manors and other assets were returned to him, although he never recovered his full influence with the Crown. He died in 1321 and the Inquest Post Mortem of the following year provided the wonderfully full description of Grove that is reproduced as Figure 10.[39] Langton's legal entanglements during his lifetime are well-recorded.[40]

Langton's importance makes it improbable that he ever lived at Grove but if he was at Chenies with Edward I at Easter 1296 he may have visited this manor then. We know the names of some of his tenants at Grove. They include William de Brianzon, John Wakewyn and possibly the Laurence de Broc whose father had been the last de Broc to own the manor.[41]

Langton's heir was Edmund Peveril. He was a minor so he held his lands initially under the custody of his mother, Alice.[42] During this period, Edward II for reasons unknown, specifically provided for Ida, the widow of John de Clinton to have use of the buildings.[43]

4 Later 14th Century, 15th & 16th Centuries: the Cheynes

by Roy and Anne Paton and Thor Harman

By 1347, Grove was back in the possession of the Crown, with the Earl of Surrey holding it for a lifetime.[44] In the course of the next fifteen years it came into the hands of Thomas Cheyne who received a grant of free warren there in 1362.[45] There had been Cheynes near Grove (at Isenhampstead Cheney, now Chenies) since before 1156[46] but Thomas came from a different branch of the family.[47] Edward III gave him many gifts and appointments.[48] These included

---

38 Camden Fourth Series 6 p.1
39 Cal I.P.M. 15 Edward II p.44
40 See amongst others McFarlane p.225 et. seq., and Camden Fourth Series 6. For Hauksherd see Camden p.211
41 Cal Close Rolls 1318-23 p.569
42 VCH III p.211
43 Ibid.
44 Cal I.P.M. 21 Edward III file 10
45 Chart. Rolls 36 Edward III p.174
46 VCH Bucks III p.200
47 Smith p.1
48 Smith p.3

making him his Shield Bearer and also Constable of Windsor Castle.[49] In 1364 the King gave Thomas rights to the manor of Drayton Beauchamp near Tring.[50] When Thomas died in 1368 those rights passed to William Cheyne who was probably his brother.[51] It appears that the ownership of Grove also passed to William because when he died in 1375 his son Roger inherited both properties.[52] Thomas and William, the first two Cheynes to be associated with Grove, can be seen commemorated in full armour in contemporary brasses in Drayton Beauchamp Parish Church[53] (see Figure 12 page 15).

When he came of age, Roger became an important man in the County and was Knight of the Shire for Buckinghamshire in the Coventry Parliament of 1404.[54] But Roger was a Lollard. Lollardy was a religious movement which, amongst other things, attacked corruption in the Church, questioned papal authority and demanded that the Bible should be available in English for everyone to read. This was, in effect, a challenge to the 'establishment' and in 1414 Roger, then aged 52, and his two sons were arrested during the Lollard Rebellion and put in the Tower.[55] Their co-religionists of lower social standing in Amersham were executed.

The Cheynes were arrested in January and Roger died in May - whether in prison or not we don't know. His son and heir John, was 24. He was pardoned in November the same year and it seems that his brother Thomas was also released.[56] John may have gone to the Holy Land soon after his pardon[57]. He became Sir John and was Sheriff of Bedfordshire and Buckinghamshire in 1423.[58] Despite this, in the next few years Sir John and Thomas terrorised the neighbourhood. By 1430, things were so bad that 'on complaint by many of the King's lieges of Hertford and Buckingham' a commission of Oyer and Terminer was issued;[59] there was a second commission to a different Commissioner the following year (see Figure 13 page 16).

The commission tells how the Cheynes had driven "divers persons from their own land" with "a strong hand", imprisoned them, made them pay fines etc,

49   Cal. Pat. Rolls (Rec. Com.) 179
50   Cal. Pat. Rolls 1364-7 23 and Smith. VCH Bucks III p.341
51   VCH III p.341
52   Smith p.8
53   RCHM Bucks South p.136
54   Smith p.9
55   Cal I.P.M. 2 Hen V file 7
56   Cal. Pat. Rolls 1413-6 p.244
57   Gibbs p.100
58   Smith p.12 and PRO List and Indices IX
59   Cal. Pat. Rolls 1429-26 p.75

and requires the Commissioner to search the manors of Grove and Drayton and to look for books and arms. This indicates that Thomas was living at Grove as he is described as being 'of Chesham' not from Drayton Beauchamp. So Grove and the present house or, at any rate, its walls, formed part of the premises searched in 1431[60]. Very probably the medieval characteristics of the site, including the remains of the 15th century gatehouses stem from the Cheynes' efforts to use the place as a stronghold by strengthening an already defensible position.

Figure 21   Cheyne Connections with Grove

```
                    ┌──────────┬──────────────┬──────────┬──────────┐
                    │          │              │          │          │
                  John    Thomas         William = Joan  Hugh      Roger
                          d 1368/9       d 1375
                                              │
                                         Roger = Agnes
                                         d 1363
                                              │
                          ┌───────────────────┴──────────┐
                   John = [1] Joan d 1466          Thomas = Ailanor
                   b 1390 d 1468 [2] Agnes d 1468         │
                                                ┌─────────┴────────┐
                                           John = Peryn         Thomas
                                           d 1459
                                                │
                                           John = Elizabeth
                                           d 1466
                                                │
                                           John = Margaret
                                           b 1466 d 1535
                                                │
                          ┌─────────────────────┼──────────────────┐
                   Robert = [1] Elizabeth    John              7 daughters
                   d 1552   [2] Mary
                          │
              ┌───────────┼──────────────────┐
           [1] John   [1] 3 daughters    [2] Thomas = [1] Elizabeth
           d 1585                                     [2] Frances
                                                │
                                            Thomas
                                            b 1560
```

Cheynes who owned Grove are shown in bold type.
Legend: [1] and [2] relate to first and second marriages and their children

---

60   Ibid. p.153 and Smith p.12

The brothers were taken to the Tower but released after a short while[61] and in 1434, like many others, they were required to take an oath 'not to maintain peacebreakers'.[62] A little earlier (by 1433) Thomas had bought Chesham Bois on the opposite side of the Chess Valley.[63] Almost ten years later he also bought Chenies which he quickly sold to his elder brother Sir John,[64] who also continued to own Grove and Drayton Beauchamp. Sir John died without issue in 1468.[65] His second wife, Agnes, survived him by 26 years. On her death, Chenies passed to her sister's daughter Anne Philip[66] whose grand-daughter married John, Earl of Bedford and so initiated the link between the house at Chenies and the Russells.

Figure 22 Sir John Cheyne was 2'0"/61cm taller than this doorway

There's a strange story about Sir John told by the Victorian antiquary Rev. Hastings Kelke, Rector of Drayton Beauchamp. It had been said that Sir John was a very big man and that he and his first wife, who died in 1445, had a son Alexander who died in infancy. Sir John was buried alongside his first wife in Drayton Beauchamp church and during the 19th century their graves were opened. Sir John was indeed found to have been a very big man, almost seven feet in height and with his wife was found buried the skeleton of a very small infant.[67] So the stories were true and little Alexander had died with his mother soon after he was born. If he had lived he would have inherited Grove. As it was, after Sir John's second wife Agnes died, Grove, which may have been leased to Aluered de Marston and John de Thwaites,[68] passed to John Cheyne of Chesham Bois, great grandson of Sir John's younger brother Thomas.

---

61 Smith p.12
62 Ibid.
63 VCH III p.219
64 Ibid. p.201
65 Chancery I.P.M. & Edward IV file 30 No 51
66 VCH p.200
67 Gibbs p.100
68 Lowndes papers Bucks CRO

John's son Robert inherited Grove, together with Chesham Bois and Drayton Beauchamp in 1535.[69] In 1544 he provided for his younger son Thomas, by arranging that he would inherit Grove.[70] He confirmed this when Thomas himself had a son (another Thomas!) in 1550.[71] Drayton Beauchamp and Chesham Bois passed to Robert's eldest son, John.

In 1577, this John struck a deal with his nephew Thomas (the child born in 1550) in which John paid Thomas £100 to assign the income of certain fields adjacent to Grove to a charity for the relief of the poor in Chesham, Amersham and Drayton Beauchamp.[72] This Thomas had interests in Bedfordshire and he sold Grove in 1578 to Thomas Southen or Southam.[73] This ended more than 200 years of ownership of Grove by the Cheyne family.

It is difficult to tell from the records exactly when the Cheyne family was resident at Grove, but details of their neighbours' complaints and of the action taken in 1430 and 1431 strongly suggest that Thomas Cheyne was then living at Grove. Certainly the finds of Cheyne sheep bells in the fields around Grove indicate that they pastured their sheep there.

5   The 17th, 18th and 19th Centuries

by Jennifer Moss

The Southens and the Bunns

Thomas Cheyne sold much of the manor of Grove to Thomas Southen[74] (or Southam) and part of it to John Partridge.[75] The land sold to Thomas Southen in 1578 is described in terms of a few large units suggesting that the later sub-division into small fields had not yet begun. Thomas Southen appears to have

---

69 Smith p.19
70 Ibid.
71 Ibid p.20
72 Chesham Parish Register, Appendix A.
73 VCH p.211
74 The Bucks County Record Office holds an extensive archive of Lowndes papers, with reference numbers all starting "D/LO". The transactions covering the period up to the first Lowndes purchase are listed in the Abstract of Title (D/LO/1/2/1-16) and for William Lowndes' Survey Roll 2 (D/LO/4/2).
Dates are frequently given in terms of the year of the sovereign's reign, so translating to dates as we know them involves taking note of when the sovereign acceded, and that until 1752 New Year's Day was May/March 25th.
The sale from Cheyne to Southen is dated 24th May 20 Eliz. ie. 1578 since Elizabeth acceded on 17 November 1558.
75 Ibid.

become the owner of the manor house and the area around it termed Grove Park. It is not clear, therefore, how John Partridge's initials came to appear on the house walls (see page 5). When Thomas Southen died the Grove property passed to his brother John and then to a William Southen.[76] There were in fact two Williams, father and son.

By 1629 the manor was in the hands of the Bunn family. In that year William Bunn conveyed all the manor except Little Grove Hill to two John Bunns, the older and younger.[77] A year later John Bunn also acquired Little Grove Hill. His will was proved in 1661[78] (one of the witnesses to the will being Seth Partridge). John's son Henry married Elizabeth Hay in 1663 and a document relating to her marriage settlement referred to other fields adjacent to Grove.[79] The Chesham Parish Register shows that nine children were born between 1664 and 1684. In 1676 Henry Bunn bought an additional 15 acres which included land that Thomas Cheyne had originally sold to John Partridge. This had descended to someone named How who sold it to John Dean less than a month before the transfer from Dean to Bunn.

In 1680 Henry Bunn appears to have started to get into financial difficulties, and he sold 22 acres to Josiah Sale.[80] After Henry's death, because Josiah Sale had not made all the payments he should have made, Henry's widow Elizabeth was able to go to court and recover the land. It was finally sold by Elizabeth and Henry's brother and nephew to William Lowndes in 1704 for £240, Josiah Sale receiving the sum of 5 shillings![81]

Henry Bunn's financial difficulties did not end with the sale of those 22 acres to Josiah Sale. He mortgaged parts of the property in 1688 and 1689 and these mortgages were not repaid before William Lowndes purchased Grove. The mortgage of 1688 tells us that Henry Bunn was indeed living at Grove because it refers to "the moat encompassing" his house.[82]

Another strand of Henry Bunn's complicated financial affairs involved a lease of the Manor for a peppercorn rent that may have arisen form Henry's failure to carry out the terms of a will of which he was executor; and a later arrangement that involved Henry Bunn agreeing to pay £30 a year to Mary

---

76   27 Sept.3 Jac 1
77   22 Aug.4 Car 1 ie. 1628
78   30 Aug.1661 (D/LO/3/5)
79   16 Nov.21 Car 2 ie. 1669 measuring from the execution of Charles I in 1649
80   29 Jan.1680 (D/LO/1/2/44)
81   17 Nov.1704 (D/LO/1/2/50)
82   10 May.4 Jac 2 ie. 1688

Wingfield throughout her life.[83] This obligation was taken on by William Lowndes when he purchased the Manor and he continued the payments during her life.

William Lowndes

In 1692 William Lowndes had the large block of land that he was to buy surveyed by Thomas Pegsworth. The results are included in the table in Appendix 2, which correlates the field names used in 1692 with those in the tithe map of 1842. William Lowndes was a stickler for accuracy, and notes that the surveyor has incorrectly summed the total of the land areas, by ten perches.[84]

It is interesting to compare the purchase price of £1,200 for these 104 acres with the £1,430 paid five years earlier by William Lowndes for The Bury estate in Chesham. The documents relating to that purchase include a valuation[85] showing how the seller George Norbury calculated the asking price of £1,500 in terms of 22 years purchase of the notional rental of each type of land. Only 46 acres were included there, and £320 was given as the value of the house etc, so the land was valued at about £1,180. There is a great difference between the notional annual rent of £2 or £3 per annum for meadows and 8 shillings or 12 shillings per acre for arable. If we take £200 as the value of the house at Grove, then £1,000 is left for the purchase price of the land, or approximately £10 per acre. If this price too was arrived at from calculating 22 years purchase of a notional rent, that sets the rent at 9 shillings per acre.[86] This suggests that the land at The Grove at this date was all, or almost all, in arable use. However, if account is taken of William Lowndes also having had to pay £483 to clear the outstanding mortgages, the cost per acre rises to about 14 shillings per acre. Since The Mead of seven acres is the only parcel clearly described as "meadow" this suggests that one or two other fields might also have been classed as meadows.

Like some previous owners of Grove (Bishop Langton in the 13th and Thomas Cheyne in the 14th century) William Lowndes was a man of some importance on the national stage. Born in 1652 in Winslow, Bucks into a family of minor gentry, he was obviously well educated, and in 1667 had moved to London to seek his fortune. By 1679 he was working at the Treasury, as a Clerk,

---

83   D/LO/1/2/24 - 28
84   D/LO/4/2.   40 perches=1 rood, 4 roods=1 acre
85   D/LO/4/6
86   Author's note: I think it is extraordinary that the cash value of the land in 1692 was almost identical to what it was in the 1920s and 1930s. Of course the value of the pound was enormously greater in William Lowndes' time, so it shows how bad the agricultural depression was between the Wars. A.S.H.

and he progressed up the Treasury ladder until in 1695, he was appointed Secretary by King William III personally. There he remained until his death in 1724, close to the changes in the way the country was governed. He was involved in the founding of the Bank of England, and as he was also elected a Member of Parliament he served as a link between the Bank and the legislature. To this day the Committee of the house of Commons that discusses finance is called the Committee of Ways and Means, and 'Ways and Means' was the motto he took when he was awarded an augmentation of his family coat of arms by Queen Anne. When he died there were fulsome tributes from Sir Robert Walpole and others.

As soon as he joined the Treasury he started to buy land, really the only investment then available. This suggests that his Treasury connections enabled him to amass considerable wealth, from salary, fees and other perquisites of office. Financial regulation in those days was not what it is today, and William was certainly able to profit from his position to a considerable extent.

His first purchases of land were all in the Winslow area, and the purchase of The Bury estate in Chesham was his first purchase elsewhere. Presumably Chesham was conveniently situated about half way to Winslow, and provided a convenient spot at which to break his journeys between London and Winslow.

Figure 23   **William 'Ways & Means' Lowndes**

The next year in which he bought land away from Winslow was 1692. In that year not only did he buy the Manor of Grove, his largest single purchase to date, but also he bought land in London. There were two purchases there, 3 acres in King Street and Carnaby Street, and the important purchase of 18 acres that would be developed by Thomas Cubitt in the 19th century as the Lowndes Knightsbridge Estate. This last purchase, for £500, he described in his Survey Roll saying that he paid this large

- 42 -

sum "for the benefit of his posterity". In other words he could envisage the long term future when the fields he bought would be developed as part of the inexorable spread of London. He was an astute man.

William Lowndes' holding at Grove was of two parcels of land, of 104 acres and 22, and each parcel was let separately for many years.

In 1698, an agreement was signed between William Lowndes (described as 'of Westminster') and Thomas Wright, for 104 acres of land already occupied by Wright to continue to be let to him at £45 per annum from Michaelmas 1698 for nine years.[87] This reserved to William Lowndes and his assignees 4½ acres of woods, and all the wood growing on the banks of the 'Mote', of some 4 acres. It also reserved all the Royalties and franchises belonging to him or them as Lord of the Manor of Grove Park, and to him and their followers and attendants liberty to hunt, hawk, fish or fowl on the land.

There were subsequent leases of the same land at the same rent, dated in 1709 (to Thomas Wright as before), 1715 (to John Wright) and 1725. The last was dated after William Lowndes' death, yet it includes his signature, and so must have been signed by him in advance of the dating of the agreement. This lease was to William Gate of Bovingdon in the county of Hertfordshire, and was to run from 'Michaelmas last past' for 12 years.[88]

The 22 acres bought in 1704 from Henry Bunn's widow, were let in 1705 to Josias Sale for 12 years and there was another agreement in 1715, the land then being let to Josias Sale Junior. At that time William Lowndes in his Survey Roll summarises his holdings in the Grove area as 1 messuage; 2 gardens; 5 orchards; 130 acres land; 5 acres meadow; 12 acres pasture; 12 acres wood. This does not quite accord with the total of 104 + 22 = 126 acres so there was an element of rounding up![89]

Rebecca Lowndes and Charles Lowndes

Under the Will of William 'Ways and Means' Lowndes his widow Rebecca had a life interest in all his Chesham estates, and they then passed to her eldest surviving son, Charles (1699-1784). It was Rebecca who signed the leases of the 22 acres to Josiah Sale in 1727 and 1740 (the year of her death)[90] Charles then signed the next lease in 1754. In all cases the rent was still £9 per annum.

---

87   D/LO/1/2/56(1)
88   D/LO/1/2/53 - 7
89   D/LO/4/2
90   D/LO/6/1/4 & D/LO/1/2/60

When Rebecca died in 1740, her youngest son Joseph administered her estate and records receiving the rents and land tax due from Mr Sale and Mr Gates.

Charles Lowndes made at least four purchases to increase the size of Grove Farm. Before 1749 he had bought two fields in the valley to the northwest of Deans Wood and one running across to Two Dells Lane. Then in 1749, 1774 and 1781 he bought further fields along Two Dells Lane.

Charles built the Great Room at The Bury and detailed accounts for this survive. In 1737 he also did work to Dungrove and Bellingdon Farms. There is reference in the accounts to payments to John Potter of £1-4-0 for drawing four loads of oak from the Great Grove to Dungrove, and 10/4 for drawing a load and 60 feet of Beech from the Grove to Dungrove.[91] So the woods at the Grove supplied timber for building work elsewhere on the Lowndes' estate in the Chesham area.

William the Commissioner of Excise and his spendthrift son

Charles Lowndes' only son, another William, served for many years as a Commissioner of Excise. This must have been a lucrative post since he paid the not inconsiderable sum of £104-7-0 as fees for the preparing of his Patent as a Commissioner.

His wife, Lydia, née Osborn, died only two years after their marriage, after giving birth to a son. He never remarried, but had two illegitimate children, given the good Lowndes names of Rebecca and Charles. He set up a trust to support them, into which he put £3,500 of Reduced Bank Annuities and £2,200 of Consolidated Bank Annuities, which gave the children and their mother an income, the capital passing to the children on reaching 21, by which time their mother, Mrs Mary Harrington, was dead.[92]

The first document relating to the Grove in this period dates from 1798, when a farm at Ashley Green is reported as assessed for Land Tax at £12-4-0, being occupied by John Barnes, and comprising 150 acres together with just over 16 acres of woods.[93] Hence the two original purchases of 104 acres and 22 acres have been again united in one title, presumably together with the additional land along Two Dells Lane, mentioned above.

---

91 D/LO/6/10/5(6)
92 D/LO/6/2/112 (1 – 26)
93 D/LO/4/21

In the early 19th century the farm, still occupied by John Barnes, is described as comprising 161 acres and 6 acres of woods, so some eleven acres of the earlier woods have been converted to arable or meadow.[94] It makes clear the six acres are 'woods and dell', somewhat larger than the woods around the banks of the moat in 1842. The other land is stated to be 150 acres arable and ten acres pasture, so no allowance is made for the actual farmhouse area, which may therefore be included in the 'woods'. The six acres of Deans Wood must have been held in hand by the Lowndes.

By this time all the Lowndes estates in the area had been put in the hands of trustees. This arose because in about 1803 William made over The Bury and other land including Grove Farm to his son by Lydia, yet another William, to "put him in a comfortable estate". This younger William proved to be something of a spendthrift. He ran up very large debts, both in London and Chesham. Many of these included what we would call conspicious consumption - the archive includes bills for fancy military uniforms for the militia he tried to raise; for huge quantities of wine; for £1,000 in Consols borrowed from a Mrs Osborn, presumably his grandmother or other relative on his mother's side. By 1806 the bills totalled in excess of £8,000 and creditors were pressing. Bankruptcy threatened. William Lowndes senior therefore set up a trust, to hold all the estates (ie. including Grove Farm where John Barnes was the tenant), pay young William a somewhat meagre allowance, and use the balance of the income to pay off the debts, with the estates ultimately passing to the younger William's eldest son.

'William the Spendthrift' obviously resented this - in his Will he refers to his eldest son already holding "the estates that ought rightfully to have been mine".[95] The son, yet another William, distinguished here as 'William the High Sheriff' since he held that office in 1848, was evidently a more sober character. He resettled the estates which continued to provide his mother with an income in her widowhood, and indeed the Lowndes Trustees held the bulk of the land until it was finally sold.

It was therefore the Lowndes Trustees who let Grove Farm to John Barnes in 1808 for eleven and a half years at £135 per annum and in 1819 for twelve years at £168 per annum.[96] In 1813 the Trustees Charles Lyall and William Sutthery also leased, at £23 per annum, a coach-house and five stall stable, stated

---

94   D/LO/4/18
95   D/LO/6/2/15 (66 + 67)
96   D/LO/6/1/14 + 21

as 'lately belonging to Grove Farm' to Frances Telk.[97] In 1831, when William the High Sheriff's father died, the farm was let to John Clare, who was already occupying it. Indeed the St Mary's Church Register of Baptisms shows that the Clares moved to Grove between March 1827, when Thomas was baptised and November 1828 when John was baptised.[98] The agreement was only for one year, following a letter to the Lowndes' solicitors, stating that he, John Clare, did not want an actual lease because of "the present state of the country" - perhaps referring to the unsettled conditions in the run-up to the Reform Bill of 1832.[99]

William High Sheriff, Squire Lowndes, and William Frith-Lowndes

The detailed information from the Censuses of 1841 to 1891[100] tells us who was living at The Grove at each Census date. Care has to be taken in that there is another John Clare in Ashley Green at some dates with an even larger farm than Grove Farm - 292 acres. In 1841 the John Clare we want is shown at Grove, aged 42, with Hannah his wife, aged 44, and six children. However in 1851, although Thomas and John are shown, then aged as would be expected 24 and 22, there is no sign of the other children. In 1841 the household also included an 18-year old maid and two agricultural labourers, aged 18 and 20. In 1851, in addition to John Clare's immediate family the household included an 8 year old nephew and two farm labourers, both aged 18. John and Hannah were still shown in the 1861 Census, when all the children had left home.

The 1842 tithe map is the first source of information on the Grove, and the other Lowndes land-holdings in the Chesham area, which enables the names of the fields to be located on the ground. The area occupied remained unchanged from the days of John Barnes' tenancy in 1798, assuming Deans Wood, which this William Lowndes had 'in hand' in 1841, was also in hand at the earlier dates.

In 1848 the last major purchase of land was made to make up Grove Farm as it remained until bought by Sydney Harman. The land bought lies at the north and north east boundary of the farm today. The abstract of title[101] shows that this land had formerly been held by one Josiah Sale (presumably a son or other descendant of the Josiah Sale who had failed to complete the 1680 purchase from Henry Bunn). Both the 1841 and 1851 Censuses show Daniel Baldwin at 'Sales', and the tithe map shows he rented 37½ acres. Although at one point the

---

97   D/LO/6/1/30
98   We are grateful to the Rev'd Roger Salsbury, Rector of Great Chesham for allowing information from the Parish Registers to be quoted here.
99   D/LO/6/1/21
100 Census Returns, Bucks – on microfilm or microfiche in Chesham Reference Library
101 D/LO/1/35/1 - 11

documents suggest only 30 acres were bought, the acreages of the individual fields listed indicate the full 37 acres were bought. At some point before the 1917 sale to Sydney Harman about 10 acres must have been sold.

Some time after 1861 Grove Farm was let to D & J Clare at a rent of £99-10-0. By the time of the First Edition of the Ordnance Survey (ie. about 1870) the map shows that the process of amalgamating small fields into large ones had started. In 1871 there is no Census entry for Grove Farm, but local directories show John Clare was still at Grove until at least 1876. By 1881 Joseph Goodson was there. He was then aged 40, and Mary his wife was 43. There was a single child, Clara aged 3, at home, and in addition there was a 14-year old general servant Martha Spicer, and two farm servants, Amos Hyde and Charles Buyen aged 16 and 14 respectively. Joseph Goodson was still there in 1891. Kelly's Directory for 1895 shows that by then Thomas Batchelor was the tenant, and in the 1899 Directory he is described as both a farmer and a pheasant breader.

The last Squire Lowndes

In 1905 old Squire Lowndes, who never married, was succeeded by his nephew William Frederick Lowndes Frith, who subsequently took the additional surname and the coat of arms of Lowndes by Royal Licence. He was known familiarly as Toby, and lived at The Bury in Chesham until the house was requisitioned by the military in World War II, when he departed and did not return after the war.

The 1910 Finance Act instituted the rating system. To implement this, a survey of land ownership known as the Domesday Survey was carried out, the results being recorded on an Ordnance Survey base. For Grove Farm almost all the information is recorded on the 1898 edition maps, a small part on the 1925 base, which must have been drawn up some time after the event.[102] The schedule shows Grove Farm occupied by Benjamin Wingrove with 194 acres of land. He had been the tenant since at least 1903. Deans Wood of 6 acres is shown once more as held in hand by William Lowndes. In 1918 the Grove was sold to Sydney Harman.

---

[102] Domesday Survey Schedule in Bucks Record Office DVD-1-116
Maps DVD-2 — XXXIX – 2, 3, 6 & 7

Appendix 1

Walter de la Grave's Two Virgates

A survey of a boundary that encompasses Grove Farm was carried out on 2nd May and 28th November 1998 by Janet Chaffey, Ian Freeman, John Gover, Marion Wells and Tim Yates of the Chess Valley Archaeological and Historical Society. Cross sections of the boundary were measured in a number of places.

The boundary defines an enclosure and consists in the most part of a ditch and a bank on its inside, and is thought to delineate the original two virgates granted in 1128 to Walter de la Grave. Although this cannot be proved, the boundary is certainly of long standing, since on all the old maps of this area, the field boundaries outside the bank and ditch do not join up with those inside.

Along the eastern side the bank and ditch has been obliterated by Grove Lane but at the north east corner, at point A (see Figure 24) they can be clearly seen. Beyond this point they have been ploughed out until the northern entrance to Grove Farm is reached at B. From here up to point C the bank and ditch are well preserved and in this stretch two cross sections were drawn. Along here the top of the bank is about one metre above the bottom of the ditch.

The boundary is lost between C and D and reappears in a well preserved state in Deans Wood where a third cross section was drawn. Throughout this length of the boundary there is a bank inside the ditch as before and also a bank on the outside of the ditch. From the top of the inside bank to the bottom of the ditch is about three quarters of a metre.

The north west corner of the enclosure has been ploughed out but its position can be extrapolated using the northern line of the ditch and the western line where it exists. A cross section was excavated and drawn at E near the north western corner as the ditch runs out of the wood into the field. The ditch was found but it was not completely excavated at the time. The soil was clay with flints and the ditch fill was loam with large flints.

Between E and G, which is at the edge of a narrow strip of woodland, the boundary has been ploughed out, but between F and G the line of the ditch could be seen in the lush grass. A fifth cross section was drawn at G. Here the top of the bank is only about half a metre above the bottom of the ditch, but inside the wood the bank survives much better where there is approximately one metre difference between the top of the bank and the bottom of the ditch. Two further cross sections were drawn in this woodland between G and H. At H the outer bank was again visible and a small secondary ditch could be seen on the inner side of the inside bank.

The southern side of the enclosure between I and J cannot be seen and would appear to be formed by a long-standing path which connects Two Dells Lane with Grove Lane.

Figure 24   Outline of boundary bank

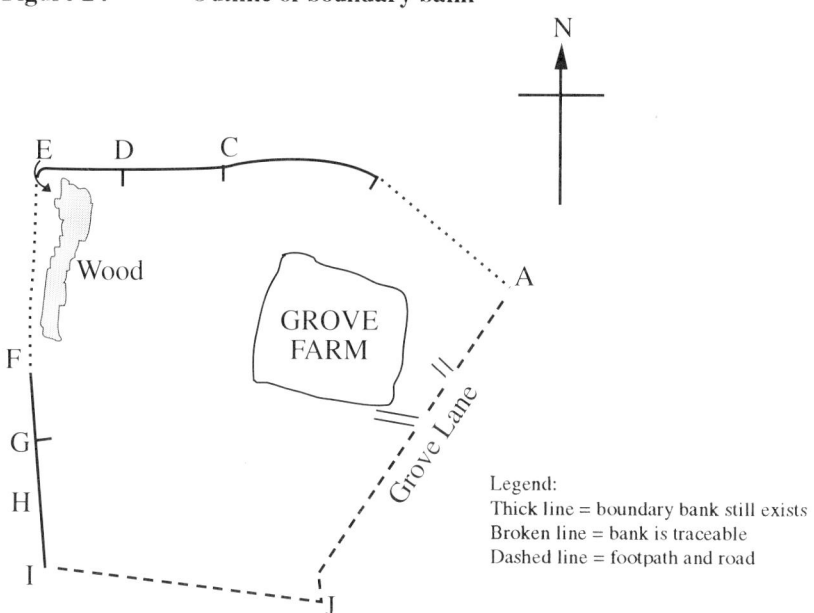

Legend:
Thick line = boundary bank still exists
Broken line = bank is traceable
Dashed line = footpath and road

Editors Note: It has not so far proved possible to rediscover the transcript in BCRO of the 1128 grant that Tony Harman saw, but Bucks FF refers (p19) to a Walter de la Grave holding one virgate and 40 acres in Chesham in 1200. This holding of a nominal 70 acres compares directly with the approximately 67 acres enclosed by the boundary discussed above. The earlier Walter is likely to have been granted two virgates (60 acres) in addition to the land he already possessed at Grove. The moated area and adjacent banks are in the region of seven acres.

Appendix 2

The Fields of Grove

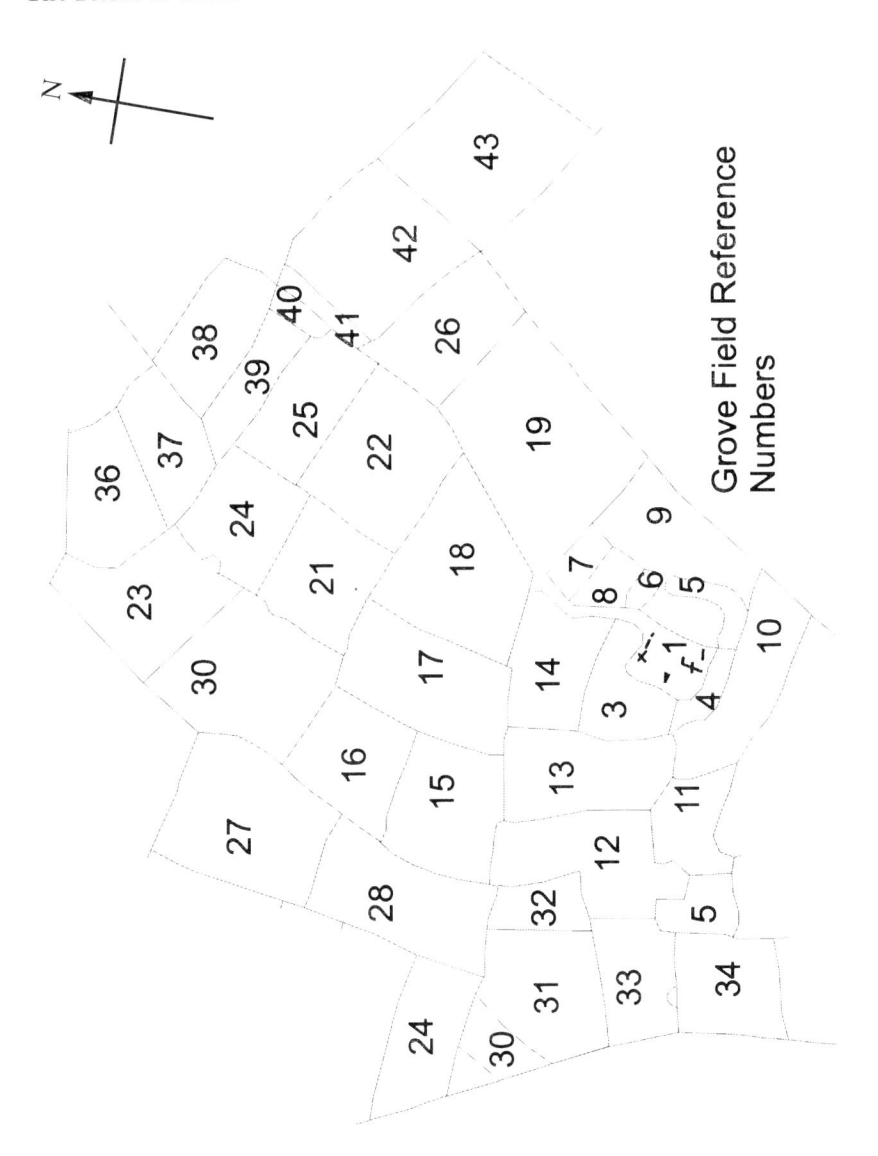

For a comparison of field names and acreages see next page.

			Purchase		Tithe Map Equivalent		1910 'Domesday' Map Acreage
	Ref.	Acreage	Name When Bought	Acreage		Name	
	1	8a	Garden etc		0a2r	House etc	2.13
	2				0a2r	Cow pasture meadow	1.58
	3 & 4			3a1r & 0a3r {		{ Banks Wood	3.92
	5 & 6			1a0r & 0a2r {		{ Wood at The Banks	1.33
	7			1a1r }		{ Hither Meadow	1.15
	8	7a	} The Meade	1a1r }	7a	{ Further Meadow	1.26
	9		}	4a2r }		{ Great Meadow	4.71
1692 Purchase	10	5a2r	Wood Close		6a	Wood Field	6.17
	11	3a	Spring Close		3a	Spring Close [incl No 35]	5.08
	12	4a	Bushy Lawn & Hill Spring		6a3r	Deans Wood (in hand)	6.51
	13	6a2r	Stock Peese		6a3r	Stock Piece	6.96
	14	4a	New Close ie recently cleared		4a2r	Rick Field & underwood	4.67
	15	7a	Hither Grove Field		6a3r	First Hanging	} 12.46
	16	5a2r	Middle Grove Field		5a2r	Middle Hanging	}
	17	7a1r	6 Acres Close		7a3r	6 acres	7.65
	18	9a	Pond Field		9a1r	Pond Field	9.52
	19	12a2r	Newlands		13a	Great Newlands	13.02
	20	9a	Further Grove Field		9a1r	Great Hanging	8.92
	21	5a	Chalk Dell Close		5a2r	Chalk Close	5.50
	22	8a	Grove Field		8a	Grove Field	8.14
		104a1r	1692 Purchase Total				
1704 Purchase	23	2a	Picket Close	} 7a1r		Stony Field	7.47
	23	5a	Stoney Close	}			
	24	5a	Dell Close		5a	Sales Dell Field & copse	5.17
	25	5a	Long Close		5a	Long Ley	5.08
	26	1a2r	Home Close & orchard	} 5a2r		Little Newlands	5.46
	26	3a	Sheepcroft	}			
		22a	1704 Purchase Total				
Bought by 1724-49	27		? Great Nuddings		9a2r	Nine Acres	9.65
	28		Lower Nuddings ?*Nether Nedle 1578*		7a2r	Bottom Field	7.44
	29				5a	Ashley Green Field	5.10
		c 22a	1724-49 Purchase Total				
Bought 1749							
	31	6a1r	Stoney Lane (Weathereds Meadow)		6a1r	Wethereds Piece [incl No 30]	7.99
Bought 1774							
	30	1a2r	Stoney Lane		1a3r	Ashley Green Meadow	[in No 31]
Bought 1781	32		Stoney Lane Pightle		2a1r	2 acre Field	2.29
	33		Stoney Lane		4a	Dell Field	8.89
	34		} Stoney Lane Hill		5a	Two Dells Field & copse	}
	35		}		1a2r	The Lagger	[in No 11]
		13a	1781 Purchase Total				
1848 Purchase	36	4a	Lithers c		4a3r	Well Field	4.83
	37	3a1r	Lithers c		3a2r	Leathers	3.51
	38	4a	Honey or Stony Croft		4a	Honey Croft	4.34
	40 & 41	0a2r	Whitehill Grove wood and house			Long orchard, garden [Sales Farm]	2.17
	39	3a2r	Pit Furlong		3a3r	Upper Leathers	3.74
	42	8a2r	Little Broadfield c		8a2r	Broad Field	8.42
	43	2a	} Hitchen	} 11a3r		Upper Broad Field	10.3
		10a1r	} Great Broadfield c	}			
		36a	1848 Purchase Total				

Notes   c - copyhold
        Purchase and 1842 areas given in acres and roods (4 roods to 1 acre), 1910 in acres only

Appendix 3
When did that happen?

This appendix shows how some of the events related to Grove fit into the historical timescale. It will also help anyone who wishes to consult original documents because for centuries these were dated by the year of the reign of the monarch – so the sale of Grove by Thomas Cheyne to Thomas Southern is dated "24 May 20 Eliz" ie 1578 since Elizabeth I acceded to the throne on 17th November 1558 (footnote 74 on p39 deals with this aspect in more detail.)

2400 BC	Beginning of Bronze Age	
800 BC	Beginning of Iron Age	Whelpley Hill camp in use
43 AD	Romans conquer Britain	
208 AD	Christianity reaches Britain	
450 AD	Saxons settle in Britain	
774 AD	Offa of Mercia described as King of the English	
878 AD	King Alfred defeats the Danes after a series of invasions and attacks by them	Danish boundary drawn close to Grove
1066 AD	Norman Conquest	Grove part of Britric's land?
1066 - 87	William I	Grove probably allocated to Hugh de Bolbec
1087 - 1100	William II	
1100 – 35	Henry I	Walter de la Grave gets 60 acres (2 virgates)
1135 – 54	Stephen	} De Brocs at Grove
1154 – 89	Henry II	} (1170 murder of
1189 – 99	Richard I	} Becket at Canterbury
1199 – 1216	John	} a de Broc involved)
1216 – 72	Henry III	} Laurence de Broc
1272 – 1307	Edward I	Hugh de Broc forfeits Grove in 1290. Edward I gives Grove to Walter Langton
1307 – 1327	Edward II	Walter Langton died 1321, inventory made
1327 – 1377	Edward III	Edward III gives Grove to Thomas Cheyne before 1362
1377 – 99	Richard II	Roger Cheyne inherits Grove 1375
1399 – 1413	Henry IV	Roger Cheyne appointed Knight of the Shire 1404

1413 – 22	Henry V	Roger Cheyne in the Tower
1422 – 61	Henry VI	John and Thomas Cheyne arrested and Grove searched 1431
1461 – 83	Edward IV	Sir John died 1468
1483 – 85	Richard III	}
1485 – 1509	Henry VII	} Cheyne
1509 – 1547	Henry VIII	} ownership
1547 – 53	Edward VI	} continues
1553 – 58	Mary	}
1558 – 1603	Elizabeth I	Thomas Cheyne sells Grove to Thomas Southen and John Partridge 1578
1603 – 25	James I	Bunn family acquire Grove
1625 – 49	Charles I	Civil War, Charles executed
1649 – 60	Commonwealth	
1660 – 85	Charles II	Henry Bunn buys 15 acres which included land sold by the Cheynes to Thomas Partridge
1685 - 88	James II	Bunn family in financial difficulties
1689 – 94	William & Mary (jointly)	William Lowndes buys Grove
1694 – 1702	William III	}
1702 – 1714	Anne	} William Lowndes and
1714 – 27	George I	} his successors build
1727 – 60	George II	} up the estate by
1760 – 1820	George III	} acquisitions of
1820 – 30	George IV	} adjacent land and let
1830 – 37	William IV	} it to tenants
1837 – 1901	Victoria	}
1901 – 10	Edward VII	}
1910 – 36	George V	Lowndes family sell Grove to Sydney Harman 1919
1936	Edward VIII	}
1936 – 52	George VI	} Harman family in
1952 on	Elizabeth II	} possession

Key to References

PRO	Public Records Office	
BCRO	Bucks County Record Office	
BRS	Bucks Record Society	
RHS	Royal Historical Society	

Barlow	"Thomas Becket" F.Barlow	University of California Press 1986
Bucks F.F.	Bucks Feet of Fines	BRS
Cal. Close R.	Calendar Close Rolls	PRO
Cal IPM	Calendar of Inquests Post Mortem	PRO
Cal Pat Rolls	Calendar of Patent Rolls	PRO
Camden	Camden 4th Series Vol 6 "Records of the Trial of Walter Langton"	PRO & RHS
Census	Census Returns Bucks (microfiche etc)	Chesham Library
Chancery IPM	Chancery Inquests Post Mortem	PRO
Chart. Rolls	Charter Rolls	PRO
Chesham Parish Register	Transcript J.W. Garret-Pegge	London 1904
D/LO	Lowndes archive	BCRO
Domesday	Domesday Book, Bucks 1086	Edn. Phillimore 1973
"Domesday"	Survey Schedule (1910 Finance Act)	BCRO
Gibbs, R.	"Worthies of Buckinghamshire"	Aylesbury 1887
Halstead, R.	"Succinct Genealogies" 1685	British Library
Indices	Historical Indices	PRO
Lowndes	Lowndes Archive	BCRO
Luffield	Luffield Priory Charters	BRS
MAC	Missenden Abbey Cartulary	BRS
McFarlane	"The Nobility of Later Medieval England"	OUP 1973
RCHM	Royal Commission on Historical Monuments – Bucks (South)	HMSO 1912
Smith, Cdr S N	"Cheyne of Drayton Beauchamp"	BCRO
Thomas K	"Religion and the Decline of Magic"	Weidenfeld & Nicholson 1971-97
VCH	Victoria County History Bucks	Constable, London 1905 etseq.

Edited	Roy Paton and Merrin Molesworth
Cover Design	Laurence Pearce
Line Drawings	Sarah Lowry, pages 1, 22 & 24

Photographs/ Illustrations			
	Ian Freeman	page	2, 27
	Roy Paton	"	5,9,28
	Nina Armour	"	6, 7, 8, 15
	Bucks Examiner	outside back cover	
	Clarissa Lewis (executor of John Piper)	"	4
	National Monuments Record	"	3
	Government Art Collection	"	42

Preparation of photographs and other illustrations	MMM Design Hawkes Design, Chesham

The author and contributors thank:

The Controller of Her Majesty's Stationery Office for permission to reproduce transcriptions of documents held in the Public Record Office.

The Rev A.W. Bennett for permission to photograph the Cheyne brasses in Drayton Beauchamp church.

They also gratefully acknowledge help received from:
        Hugh Hanley

and the staff of   The British Library
                          The Public Records Office
                          The Buckinghamshire County Record Office
                          Chesham Library